DRIVE WITH ME TO: CALIFORNIA DMV HANDBOOK

350+ DRIVING QUESTIONS TO PRACTICE AND HELP YOU PASS YOUR DRIVING EXAM TEST

DRIVERSLAND

CONTENTS

LEAVE A QUICK REVIEW!

We would like to give a big thanks to our supporters—
whoever read the book! If you enjoyed the book, please
leave a review or rating on Amazon!

If you want to get access or news about our new books
or be part of a great community, please Scan the QR
Code below and like our page on Facebook!

ABOUT THE AUTHOR

Who are we:

Driversland comprises a team of experienced and astute professional driver instructors, teachers, auto driving trainers, educators, and truck driving trainers who are motivated by the dream of promoting safe driving practices among road users. We aim to publish books on the topic of driving to teach and train people about road safety measures. With forty years of experience in this field, we have published a variety of great pieces on this topic for our diverse pool of readers who are studying for the DMV driving license in the state of California. We are passionate about sharing our experiences and skills with future generations, and our target is every individual who desires to learn and acquire safe driving skills. Our future goal is to open our driver instructor school where we will continue offering these services, a dream to which we commit ourselves every day.

ROAD SIGNS

1. The symbol signifies:

    A. No turning around.
    B. Ahead is a traffic light.
    C. Railroad in front.

According to this notice, the right answer is A. U-turns are not permitted.

2. When you see this black and yellow sign, it means:

A. Only one-way driving is allowed on the road to the right.

B. Due to road work, there is a diversion to the right.

C. The road ahead abruptly turns in a different direction.

The right answer is C. Yellow warning signs often have black writing. You are warned of impending situations by them. Drivers are advised to slow down and brace themselves for a sudden, sharp turn on the road.

3. This sign means:

    A. Side street.
    B. Merge.
    C. Give way to traffic.

The right answer is A. This sign warns of an upcoming junction with a side road.

4. From top to bottom, the following is the proper order for traffic lights:

A. Red, yellow, green.
B. Red, green, yellow.
C. Green, red, yellow.

The right answer is A. Yellow warning signs often have black writing. You are warned of impending situations by them. This sign informs motorists that an upcoming crossroads will have traffic lights.

5. This sign means:

    A. Give way to traffic.
    B. No zone for passing.
    C. A narrowing of lanes

The right answer is A. You must yield the right-of-way if you see a triangular red and white sign.

6. This sign means:

A. People are strolling down the road in front of them.
B. Up ahead is a pedestrian crossing.
C. Crossing here by foot is not permitted.

The right answer is B. Yellow warning signs often have black writing. Drivers are warned by this sign where pedestrians might be crossing. Drivers are required to stop and remain stopped until the pedestrian leaves the crosswalk if they see one of these signs marking a pedestrian crossing.

7. An orange and red triangular sign on a vehicle always mean:

    A. Right-of-way belongs to the car.
    B. The vehicle is traveling slowly.
    C. Look forward to your job.

The right answer is B. Slow-moving vehicles have an orange and red triangle on the rear, including farm tractors, vehicles used for road maintenance, and carts driven by animals.

8. This sign means:

A. You need to go to the right lane and slow down.

B. If you are moving more slowly than the rest of the traffic, stay in the right lane.

C. The right exit is required for slower traffic.

The right answer is B. You must follow vital guidelines according to a white, rectangular notice. This sign instructs motorists to keep the left lane free for passing and quicker vehicles whenever feasible.

9. When you see this sign:

A. You are close to a railroad crossing and must be ready to stop.
B. Always come to a stop at the approaching railroad crossing.
C. You should not cross the train lines without first stopping and waiting for a signal.

The correct answer is A. This sign warns you that a railroad crossing is ahead. You must see, hear, move more slowly, and be ready to stop. Before moving forward, watch for any passing trains.

10. This sign means:

A. Not a right turn.
B. With care, a right turn is authorized at a red light.
C. At the next junction, all vehicles must turn right.

The right answer is A. A black symbol with a red circle and a diagonal line above it signifies that the activity it represents is forbidden. In this instance, the sign says it is not permitted to turn right.

11. This sign means:

A. Don't go in.
B. Give way to traffic.
C. Parking spaces are aside for those with impairments.

The right answer is A. This sign is put on one-way streets and other roads where vehicles are not permitted to enter. If a car attempts to join an expressway ramp from the wrong direction, they may notice this sign.

12. This road sign means:

    A. A junction is up ahead.
    B. Traffic is combining.
    C. Ahead is a steep slope.

The right answer is C. Warning signs, often yellow with black markings, alert drivers to situations that may not be immediately obvious. This warning sign alerts motorists to an impending steep incline. To prevent crashes and brake damage, drivers should modify their speed as necessary.

13. This yellow sign means:

A. Railways are under control in front.
B. If the light flashes, be ready to halt.
C. A traffic light is up ahead.

The right answer is C. There is a traffic light up ahead, as indicated by a yellow sign with an image of one. Be ready to react when the next traffic light appears.

14. This sign means:

    A. Don't go in.
    B. To stop.
    C. Construction or upkeep is going on.

The correct answer is C. The orange diamond-shaped signs identify construction, maintenance, survey, and utility work zones. These signs aid in guiding pedestrians and automobiles safely through hazardous areas. In the regions indicated by these signs, fines for traffic violations may double.

15. This sign means:

A. Incoming yield sign.
B. A side street is coming in from the left.
C. Stop sign in front.

The right answer is A. This sign warns drivers that a yield sign is coming up. When you notice this cautionary message, you should start to slow down.

16. This sign indicates the road ahead:

    A. Abruptly turns right, then left.
    B. Turns right before turning left.
    C. Has a rightward curve.

The right answer is B. This sign alerts drivers of a reverse bend when the road turns right before turning left.

17. This road sign means:

    A. Right-lane vehicles must reduce their speed.
    B. No turning left.
    C. Merge.

The right answer is C. Yellow warning signs often have black writing. According to this notice, vehicles may be merging safely from the right. Therefore drivers should be ready to do so.

18. This sign shows one type of:

    A. Intersection.
    B. Road bend.
    C. A right turn.

The right answer is A. Yellow warning signs often have black writing. You are warned of impending situations by them. This notice cautions drivers that a road will soon cross before them.

19. This sign shows one type of:

    A. A right turn
    B. Intersection.
    C. Lane shift.

The right answer is B. Yellow warning signs often have black writing. This sign informs you that the route you're traveling terminates at a junction up ahead. Before making a right or left turn, slow down and be ready to yield or halt.

20. This white sign means:

A. There are controls at the train crossing.
Continue moving at your normal speed.
B. Search, hear, and be ready to stop at the
crossing if required.
C. Wait for a signal before crossing the train
tracks.

The right answer is B. You must look, listen, slow down, and be ready to stop as you approach a railroad crossing. Before moving forward, let any trains pass.

21. This sign means:

A. This lane allows for movement in either direction.
B. Two-way traffic is present.
C. A split roadway is about to come into view.

The right answer is B. Two-way traffic is indicated by this sign.

22. This traffic sign denotes:

    A. Ahead, the road becomes wider.
    B. Lane narrowing and as the right lane closes,
    motorists should merge to the left.
    C. Ahead is a highway entry ramp.

The right answer is B. Typically, a warning sign is yellow with black writing. This sign warns that there will be fewer lanes up ahead and that motorists must merge to the left.

23. This sign means:

    A. Pedestrian overpass.
    B. Side street.
    C. Railroad in front.

The right answer is A. There is a crossing for pedestrians, according to this sign.

24. This road sign means:

    A. Straight ahead, a sharp right bend.
    B. A sharp turn to the left and the right.
    C. The road ahead is winding.

The right answer is C. Yellow warning signs often have black writing. This notice forewarns the motorist that a twisting route is coming up. Speed has to be set properly.

25. This sign means:

    A. Trucks are moving in.
    B. Just for trucks.
    C. A steep descent is coming.

The right answer is C. This sign alerts drivers of an impending steep descent. Drivers should check the brakes.

26. What does this road sign mean?

    A. A winding path.
    B. Gravel in sections.
    C. When wet, slippery.

The right answer is C. This warning warns drivers that damp conditions might make the road slippery. Driving on a slippery road requires care.

27. This sign means:

A. Bends forward.
B. The beginning of a divided roadway.
C. The end of a divided roadway.

The right answer is C. Yellow warning signs often have black writing. The split roadway finishes up ahead, according to this sign. Get ready to change lanes or position in a lane.

28. This yellow warning sign means:

A. You are nearing a crosswalk or a school.
B. Drive cautiously, go slowly, and keep an eye out for kids.
C. The above two things.

The right answer is C. This sign is put up on highways close to schools to alert drivers to slow down, drive cautiously, and keep an eye out for kids.

29. When you see this sign, you should stop and:

A. Only look for cars in the direction you want, then continue.

B. Let all oncoming or departing cars go ahead of you.

C. Before moving forward, check for traffic going in all directions.

The right answer is C. You must stop completely at a stop sign and look both ways for oncoming traffic before continuing.

30. This sign means:

    A. No one may enter.
    B. There's no parking.
    C. You can't stop.

The right answer is A. No one may enter. This road sign, which reads "No Entry," designates a route off-limits to illegal vehicles.

2

KNOWLEDGE

QUESTIONS AND ANSWERS

1. In which of the following scenarios should your wheels not be pointed straight ahead?

    A. While awaiting a left turning at such a stop sign.
    B. When driven on a sloped driveway or hill.
    C. When stopped in the front of an open, level road without a curb.

The right answer is B. Keep your wheels pointing straight ahead while you wait to make a left turn until it is safe. This will keep you from swerving into oncoming traffic if a car strikes you from behind. Turn the wheels while parking uphill or downhill to prevent the car from rolling into oncoming traffic if the brakes fail.

2. When driving in fog, rain, or snow, use:

    A. Little beams.
    B. Tall beams.
    C. Just fog lights.

The right answer is A. Low laser headlights should be utilized in the rain, snow, and fog. Under severe weather circumstances, the light from hazard lights will bounce back to the driver, creating a glare that will make it very difficult to see in front of the vehicle.

3. If a truck or bus is making a right turn where you also need to make a right turn, you should:

A. Turn quickly first before the truck or bus can.
B. Wait for the vehicle or bus to make its turn before turning.
C. Squeeze in between the curb and the truck or bus.

The right answer is B. You risk suffering a major collision if you attempt to squeeze your car between another reversing truck or bus and a curb. Do not turn till the truck or bus has finished its turn to prevent a collision.

4. You should increase the distance between your vehicle and the vehicle ahead when you:

A. Are pursuing a compact passenger car.
B. Are being followed closely by another motorist.
C. Are exceeding the posted speed while driving.

The right answer is B. When tailgating, leave more room in front of your car and avoid braking abruptly. To avoid colliding with the tailgater, slow down or go into another lane.

5. When driving under snowy or icy conditions:

A. Utilizing your cruise control is secure.
B. Change your direction and speed more gently than you normally would.
C. Drive normally as you would in other situations.

The right answer is B. You should gradually modify your speed and direction while driving on snowy or slippery roads. When traveling on snow or ice, never use cruise control since your tires might lose traction, and you could lose control of your car.

6. A broken yellow centerline means that:

A. Passing is prohibited.
B. When the path ahead is clear, overtaking on the left is allowed.
C. You may pass on the left when there is no obstruction in your path.

The correct answer is C. If there is no oncoming traffic, a motorist may cross the median to overtake a vehicle just on the left if the yellow centerline is broken. A driver should never cross a solid yellow median to pass.

7. Which of these statements is true about changing lanes?

A. You merely need to turn and glance over your right leg to check for left- or right-lane changes.
B. If you notice a change in lanes, look over your shoulder first and then over your left.
C. Blind spots are not present in a vehicle with two front mirrors.

The right answer is B. Signal before reversing lanes. To help ensure the lane next to you is free, check all your mirrors and peek over your left or right shoulder. One approach to ensure there isn't a car in your blind area is to look over your shoulder. Traffic on a motorbike or a bicycle in the lane ahead.

8. When being followed by a tailgater, which of the following will help you avoid being hit from behind?

A. Switching to a different lane.
B. Reducing the distance you follow.
C. Frequently switching lanes.

The right answer is A. If a driver is tailgating you, you should gradually slow down or move into another lane to avoid a crash.

9. If you approach a traffic light with a red signal and a police officer directs you to go through the intersection without stopping, you should:

A. Stop as soon as the light turns red.
B. Pass past the junction without pausing.
C. Come to a full halt before moving forward.

The right answer is B. Police personnel directing traffic are always allowed to overrule official traffic signals and signage. Take the officer's instructions to heart.

10. Which of the following factors affect an individual's absorption of alcohol?

A. Weight.
B. Height.
C. Intelligence.

The right answer is A. The quantity of food in someone's stomach, their weight, their sexual identity, and how many alcoholic drinks they've had all impact how much alcohol they absorb. The only way to get alcohol out of someone's system would be to wait.

11. Fatigue Increases the risk of:

A. Missing a doorway.

B. Missing an appointment.

C. Collision after nodding off while driving.

The right answer is C. Your danger of getting in a collision rises, and your decision-making process becomes slower due to fatigue mistakes relating to speed and distance. If you are worn out, you risk falling asleep at the wheel, crashing, and hurting or killing other people.

12. Which of the following blocks the smooth flow of traffic?

A. Moving more slowly to inspect the crash site.

B. Preventing pointless lane changes.

C. Instead of driving, use public transit.

The right answer is A. Rubbernecking, which involves slowing down to observe crashes or other unusual phenomena, increases traffic jams and should be avoided.

13. You want to make a right turn at an upcoming intersection. You need to slow down, right?

    A. Take a step to the left in your lane.
    B. Stay out of the bicycle lane while driving.
    C. Before turning, provide a 100-foot signal.

The right answer is C. You should start flashing your lights around 100 feet before a right turn.

14. When driving in work zones, you should:

    A. Pass through the zone as fast as possible and pick up the pace.
    B. Reduce your velocity and be ready to stop abruptly.
    C. Pass through the zone and keep moving at your usual pace.

The right answer is B. Slow down and is ready to halt while entering and traveling through a work zone. Respect the stated speed restrictions and pay attention to your surroundings. There could be workers there.

15. When backing up:

A. View out the back window.

B. Step here on the gas pedal firmly.

C. Just use the rearview mirror.

The right answer is A. Place your right hand on the backrest of the back seat as you begin to reverse and stare straight out the back windshield. Do not rely on your side or rearview mirrors since they do not display what is immediately behind your car. The reverse should only be used at a slow pace.

16. You are approaching an intersection at the posted speed limit when the signal turns yellow. You ought to:

A. Pass past the junction without being cautious while moving slowly.

B. Go quickly through the junction well before the light turns red.

C. Stop before going through the junction if you can safely do so.

The right answer is C. When the light is solidly yellow, it symbolizes "caution" and warns that it will soon become red. If it's safe to do so, you may stop at such a solid yellow light; otherwise, you should proceed with caution while crossing the junction.

17. A person may legally ride in the back of a pickup truck when:

  A. The truck bed's sidewalls are at least twenty-four inches tall.
  B. A camper shell is attached to the pickup's rear.
  C. Using an authorized safety belt in a fastened seat.

The right answer is C. You should never let anybody ride in the back of the truck or other truck unless they are using both the seat and a safety belt.

18. Which of these statements is true about drugs and driving?

  A. If you don't feel sleepy, using any prescription medication is safe.
  B. Even over-the-counter medications might make you unable to drive.
  C. Only illicit substances can make you unable to drive.

The right answer is B. Legal pharmaceutical and over-the-counter medications, including those used to treat colds, hay fever, allergens, or to relax nerves or muscles, might make it difficult for you to drive. Any substance that makes it impossible for you to drive safely is prohibited from using while driving; this legislation does not distinguish between illicit, prescription, and over-the-counter medicines.

19. When you are behind a motorcycle, you should:

A. Have your horn at the ready.
B. Increase your speed.
C. Give yourself more room to follow.

The right answer is C. Allow at least a ranging from two to four distances while following a biker. Following a motorcycle too closely puts both your life and the motorcyclist's life at risk since they might stop suddenly. Therefore, you need to provide adequate space in case the rider falls. There is a higher risk of falling on wet and slippery roads, gravel driveways, and metal like bridges, gratings, and tram or railroad tracks.

20. When driving at night on a dimly lit street, you should:

A. Drive so that you may stop inside the area where your headlights illuminate.
B. Turn on the high beam headlights to see the cars in front of you more clearly.
C. Keep the OLED panel lights bright to be more apparent to other drivers.

The right answer is A. Because it is harder to see far forward at night than during the day, you should travel more slowly. Make sure you can stop in the area where your headlights are illuminating.

21. You are approaching a green traffic light, and traffic is blocking the intersection. What is the best thing to do?

A. Establish your right-of-way by partially approaching the junction.
B. Wait until you can cross entirely before proceeding through the junction.
C. Wait, allow traffic to pass before proceeding into the junction.

The right answer is B. You must avoid entering an intersection even if your light is green unless you can pass through it entirely before the signal turns red. You may get a citation if you obstruct the junction.

22. When being passed by another vehicle:

A. Brake firmly.
B. Keep your pace steady.
C. Hurry up.

The right answer is B. When being overtaken, you must slow down and give way to the oncoming car. Permit the car to safely enter your lane.

23. Two traffic lanes are moving in your direction. You are driving in the left lane, and many vehicles pass you on the right. If the driver behind you wishes to drive faster, you should:

A. Stay in your lane to avoid impeding the flow of traffic.
B. Go to the left shoulder to allow other cars to pass.
C. Move into the right-hand lane when it is appropriate to do so.

The right answer is C. Use the left lane to go swiftly, pass, or make a left turn. At the same time, approaching the road, make a right turn, or travel more slowly than the traffic ahead.

24. Yellow lines separate:

A. One-way roadways with traffic lanes.
B. On two-way roadways, there is traffic traveling in the opposing direction.
C. From all normal traffic lanes to the carpool lanes.

The right answer is B. Yellow lines indicate a two-way road's center. Drivers are not permitted to cross a solid yellow median to pass. Drivers may cross a broken yellow median to pass, only if doing so would not impede other traffic.

25. The driver ahead of you stops at a crosswalk. What should you do?

A. Pass the car slowly, no faster than 10 mph.
B. Once every pedestrian has crossed, stop and only continue.
C. Change lanes, take a close look, and pass the stationary automobile.

The right answer is B. A car that is halted at a crosswalk cannot be passed. You may not be able to notice any pedestrians crossing the roadway. Instead, halt and only go forward after every pedestrian has crossed.

26. If you are about to be hit from the rear, you should not:

    A. Let go of your seatbelt.
    B. Prepare to stand.
    C. Place your head firmly against the headrest.

The right answer is A. Your body will be flung backward if your car is struck from behind while you are moving ahead. To avoid whiplash, brace yourself by squeezing the back of the seat and resting your head on the head restraint. To prevent being pushed into yet another car, hold the steering column firmly and be prepared to hit the brakes.

27. Drivers must use their seat belts:

    A. Unless they are operating a car that was made before 1978.
    B. Unless they are a limousine driver.
    C. And if you don't, you'll get a traffic penalty.

The right answer is C. Drivers who fail to buckle up are subject to fines if they do not.

28. If you park facing uphill on a street with a curb, set the parking brake and:

A. The front wheels toward the direction of the curb.
B. Turn the front wheels away from the curb.
C. The front wheels should remain straight.

The right answer is B. Your wheels must be pointed away from the ground while parking downhill on a street with a curb. Your tires should be pointed toward to curb or edge of a road while parking uphill or downhill on a roadway without a curb.

29. The driver ahead of you stops at a crosswalk. What should you do?

A. Pass the car slowly, no faster than 10 mph.
B. Once every pedestrian has crossed, stop and only continue.
C. Change lanes, take a careful look and pass the stationary automobile.

The right answer is B. A car that is halted at a crosswalk cannot be passed. You may not be able to notice any people crossing the roadway. Stop instead, and only go forward when every pedestrian has crossed.

30. If you are about to be hit from the rear, you should not:

    A. Let go of your seatbelt.
    B. Prepare to stand.
    C. Place your head firmly against the headrest.

The right answer is A. Your torso will be flung backward if your car is struck from behind while moving forward. To avoid whiplash, brace yourself by squeezing the back of your seat and resting your head on the head restraint. To prevent being forced into another car, have a firm hold on the wheel and be prepared to hit the brakes.

31. Drivers must use their seat belts:

    A. Unless they are operating a car that was made before 1978.
    B. Unless they are a limousine driver.
    C. And if you don't, you'll get a traffic penalty.

The right answer is C. Drivers who fail to buckle up are subject to fines if they do not.

32. If you park facing uphill on a street with a curb, set the parking brake and:

  A. The front wheels toward the direction of the curb.
  B. Turn the front wheels away from the curb.
  C. The front wheels should remain straight.

The right answer is B. Your wheels must be pointed away from the building while parking downhill on a street with a curb. Your wheels should be pointed toward the curb or border of the road while parking uphill or downhill on a roadway without a curb.

33. A solid yellow line on your side of the centerline means:

  A. Speed up a little.
  B. A traffic light ahead.
  C. Pass no more.

The right answer is C. On two-lane roadways, solid yellow lines denote areas where passing is forbidden. Drivers in the lane closest to a solid yellow line may not pass if one appears adjacent to a broken yellow line. Both yellow lines would be solid in rare cases, signifying that passing from either direction is unsafe.

34. Which of the following is a dangerous habit when driving in work zones?

A. Pursuing a vehicle too closely.
B. Failing to keep a close eye out for employees and moving machinery.
C. The above two things.

The right answer is C. Adjust your pace for the traffic situation and avoid following other cars too closely while driving through a construction zone. Pay close attention to the people and equipment in the work area.

35. When passing, you should move back into the right lane when:

A. You are one car length in front of the one that just passed.
B. You can make out both lights of the passing car in your rearview mirror.
C. The passing car is 50 feet in front of you.

The right answer is B. Pass only when you have adequate room to return to the driving lane. Make sure you have adequate space between you and the car you passed before moving back into the driving lane. It is okay to go back in the driving lane once you can see both lights of the passing car in your rearview mirror.

36. It is necessary to use your low beams any time you are:

A. On a roadway that is lit.
B. On the highway.
C. In fog.

The right answer is C. When traveling in fog, snow, drizzle, or mist, use your low lights. Precipitation will reflect the intense beams of light, creating brightness and making seeing even more challenging. Some cars come with fog lights, which you should use instead of your low beam headlights.

37. Reaction time is slower after:

A. Consuming alcohol.
B. Sleeping.
C. Striving hard.

The right answer is A. Alcohol impairs your reflexes and reaction times, blurs your vision, and dulls your sense of alertness. Your judgment becomes poorer, and you lose the ability to drive as your blood alcohol level rises. You'll have difficulty estimating distances, speeds, and how other cars are moving.

38. Before returning to your original lane after passing another vehicle, you should:

A. Make a horn noise.
B. In your rearview mirror, observe both headlights of the passing car.
C. Flash headlights.

The right answer is B. Check your rearview mirror for both of the passing vehicle's headlights when passing is allowed. Then you may safely switch back to your old lane.

39. When approaching a person who is crossing the street while using a white cane or guide dog, you should:

A. Stop when the individual is far enough from your route of travel.
B. Honk your horn as you pass them.
C. Drive around them with caution.

The right answer is A. You must stop when you get close to a person crossing the street with a white cane or a guiding dog and wait until they are far outside your direction of travel. Give way to blind people at all times.

40. When driving behind another vehicle at night, you should:

A. Maintain the low brightness setting on your headlights.
B. Use your bright headlights until you are 10 feet from the car in front.
C. Use the high beams on your headlights.

The right answer is A. When traveling in rural regions or with no other vehicles, just use your high beam headlights. When closely pursuing another vehicle, switch your headlamps to the low beam position.

41. Which child would require a child passenger restraint system?

A. 4 feet 10 inches tall and nine years old.
B. A 5 feet 3 inch ten-year-old boy.
C. A 4 foot 8 inches tall seven-year-old.

The right answer is C. Children must be eight years old and taller than 4 feet 9 inches to wear a safety belt that complies with federal regulations. A child passenger restraints device must be used to confine any additional youngsters.

42. When you tailgate other drivers (drive close to their rear bumper):

A. The other drivers might get irate and frustrated with you.
B. No traffic ticket may be issued as a consequence of your activities.
C. By easing the gridlock on the streets.

The right answer is A. Tailgating is the primary factor in most rear-end incidents. Use the "three-second rule" to stop tailgating. Count "one-thousand-one, one-thousand-two, one-thousand-three" when the car in front of you passes a certain location, such as a sign. You are going way too fast if you cross the same location before you have finished counting.

43. If your cell phone rings while driving and you do not have a hands-free device, you should:

A. Take the call in case there is an emergency.
B. Leave a voicemail for the caller.
C. Double-check the caller's number before you answer the phone.

The right answer is B. Without a hands-free device, drivers shouldn't use their cellphones. Except in an emergency, using a mobile phone while driving is forbidden for children. It is advised that you will let calls go over to voicemail while driving to avert distractions, even if you do have a palms device.

44. Should you always drive more slowly than other traffic?

A. No, driving too slowly may cause traffic jams.
B. The answer is that it's a wise defensive driving tactic.
C. Yes, driving slower than other traffic is usually safer.

The right answer is A. You must drive slower than usual when there is heavy traffic or terrible weather. However, if you drive too slowly and obstruct acceptable and regular traffic flow, you might get a ticket.

45. If you must park your vehicle in an area not usually used for parking:

A. Turn on your reverse lights as you park.
B. Ensure that cars coming from any angle can see your car.
C. Five yards from the curb is par.

The right answer is B. After being parked, drivers are in charge of ensuring their cars do not turn dangerous. Make sure your automobile is visible to traffic coming from any direction wherever you park.

46. When a school bus is stopped on the road ahead to load or unload children, you must:

A. Come to a full stop till every youngster has gotten off the bus.
B. Stop completely until the cease arm is released and the red lights stop blinking.
C. Alternate lanes, and proceed carefully as you pass the bus.

The right answer is B. When a bus is halted in front of you with its stop arms outstretched and lights flashing, you should come to a full stop and wait to go forward until the stop arm has been retracted and the lights have ceased flashing. Continue to wait until you are certain no kids are crossing the road in front of you after the bus starts to move again.

47. Unless otherwise posted, the speed limit in a residential area is:

A. 20 mph.
B. 25 mph.
C. 30 mph.

The right answer is B. Unless otherwise indicated, the commercial and residential areas have a 25 mph speed restriction.

48. Which of the statements is true about drinking alcohol and driving?

A. It is okay to drive after drinking if you really can walk straight.
B. Driving is not affected if your blood alcohol level is below the legal limit.
C. Alcohol impairs judgment, which is necessary for safe driving.

The right answer is C. Your judgment is impacted by alcohol use. Good judgment is required to respond effectively to things you see or hear when driving. Any quantity of alcohol consumption is likely to impair your ability to drive safely, even if your blood alcohol level is below the legal limit.

49. Vehicles stopped behind a school bus with its red lights flashing must remain stopped until:

A. Every pupil exited the bus.
B. The stop arm has retracted.
C. The bus starts moving again after the retraction of the stop arm.

The right answer is C. Drivers must come to a complete stop while a bus is flashing its red lights but has its stopping arm extended until the lights are switched off, the stop arm is retracted, and the bus starts moving again.

50. You're driving in the far right lane of a four-lane freeway and notice thick broken white lines on the left side of your lane. Are you driving in?

A. The carpool track and the following lane must combine.
B. A dedicated lane for automobiles traveling slowly.
C. An entrance lane.

The right answer is C. Large lower section painted on the ground often indicates the end of a freeway lane. Be ready to leave the motorway or for the lane to end if you are traveling in a lane with these broken lines.

51. You see a flashing yellow traffic signal at an upcoming intersection. What does the flashing yellow light mean?

A. Stop before proceeding through the crossing if it's safe to do so.
B. Stop. Before crossing the crossroads, give way to any oncoming cars.
C. Cross the crossing slowly and with caution.

The right answer is C. You are advised to proceed cautiously toward a flashing yellow signalized intersections light. Before approaching the crossing, go slowly and pay attention. If any automobiles, bicycles, or pedestrians are at the junction, yield to them.

52. If you drive more slowly than the flow of traffic, you will most likely:

A. Get a citation for interfering with traffic.
B. Boost the flow of traffic.
C. Drive defensively while demonstrating.

The correct answer is A. You must travel more slowly than normal when there is heavy traffic or terrible weather. However, if you drive too slowly and obstruct acceptable and regular traffic flow, you might get a ticket. Unless the traffic moves faster than the posted speed limit, you should keep up with it.

53. You may drive a motor vehicle in a bike lane:

A. If your speed is less than 15 mph.
B. Before turning the right turn, go no upwards of 200 feet.
C. Whenever there aren't any bikers around.

The right answer is B. You may enter this bicycle lane if you're making a right turn no more than 200 feet well before the corner or driveway. At any other moment, motor vehicle drivers shouldn't enter a bicycle lane.

54. Give the right-of-way to any pedestrian who is:

A. In a designated crosswalk.
B. In any junction or crosswalk.
C. In any street crossing.

The right answer is C. When crossing the roadway at a marked or unmarked crosswalk, drivers are required to yield to pedestrians. Drivers should give way to pedestrians crossing any roadway out of consideration for their safety.

55. The California "Basic Speed Law" says you must:

A. Keep your pace in line with the flow of other vehicles.
B. Never drive more quickly than is safe under the circumstances.
C. Follow the stated speed limit at all times.

The right answer is B. According to the "Basic Speed Law," you should never travel faster than is secure under the circumstances. Even if you are going slower than the official speed limit, you might still get a ticket for driving "too fast for the circumstances" if you travel at maximum speed in a 55-mph zone through a thick fog.

56. You should allow an extra cushion of space:

A. While driving behind a station wagon.
B. While driving behind someone whose rearview mirror is obscured.
C. When a little passenger automobile is being followed.

The right answer is B. If you follow closely behind a truck, bus, van, or any other vehicle towing a camper or trailer, they may not be unable to see you. When driving around one of these cars, widen your following distance. Reduce your distance so you can look around both sides of the vehicle and see the road ahead since huge vehicles may also obscure your vision of the road.

57. When driving on a multilane street with two-way traffic:

A. Follow closely behind other cars so that drivers may see you.
B. Drive either in front of or behind some other cars.
C. Driving in the lane closest to the center line is the safest option.

The right answer is B. If another motorist fills your area or attempts to change the wrong lane, driving closely next to them might result in an accident. You should avoid passing cars in other lanes, either in front of or behind them.

58. U-turns in residential districts are legal:

    A. On a green signal on a one-way roadway.
    B. While no close-moving vehicles are in sight.
    C. Along with sets of double solid yellow lines.

The right answer is B since U-turns are allowed in residential zones if no cars approach within 200 feet. Additionally, they are allowed when a road sign, light, or signal shield you from oncoming cars.

59. Which of these vehicles must always stop before crossing railroad tracks?

    A. Placards for hazardous materials are shown
    on tank trucks.
    B. A boat trailer is being towed by a pickup truck
    or an RV.
    C. Any car weighing greater than 4,000 pounds
    and having three or more axles.

The right answer is A. Before crossing railroad rails, trucks carrying hazardous cargo must halt.

60. If the double yellow line is near another vehicle, may you cross it to pass it?

If the road's opposite side is marked with a solid line.

A. If it's a broken line on your side of a street.
B. If the line on the opposite side of the street is broken.

The right answer is B. If a broken line is close to your driving lane, triple yellow lines inside the middle of the road signal that you may pass.

61. If you encounter an aggressive driver, you should:

A. Confront them.
B. Leave them alone.
C. Hurry up.

The right answer is B. To keep the peace and prevent accidents, drivers must consider all other road users, collaborate with them, and follow certain laws. It is best to move out of the path if you meet an aggressive motorist. Always stay out of other drivers' races.

62. Water on the road can cause a vehicle to hydroplane. Your car may hydroplane at speeds as low as:

A. 45 mph.
B. 35 mph.
C. 40 mph.

The right answer is B. When there is ponding on the road, hydroplaning happens. Most tires will direct water away first from the tire due to its effects at 35 mph. Beyond 35 mph, your tires won't be able to channel that water as efficiently, and you risk losing control of your vehicle and having it ride over the water like a pair of water skis.

63. If you are convicted of driving with an excessive blood alcohol concentration (BAC), you may be sentenced to serve:

A. A prison term of up to six months.
B. A prison term of up to twelve months.
C. No prison term, but a 500 USD fee is required.

The right answer is A. If you are found guilty of DUI for the first time and have a high BAC, you might get a sentence of up to six years in prison and a fine ranging from 390 USD to 1,000 USD. Your car can be seized, and storage costs apply.

64. You may not park your vehicle:

A. In an emergency, on the shoulder of the road.
B. Next to a curb with red paint.
C. One hundred feet or less from an elementary school.

The right answer is B. A red-painted curb does not allow for stopping, standing, or parking. Buses may, however, halt in a red bus-only curb zone.

65. If you have trouble seeing other vehicles because of dust or smoke blowing across the roadway, you should drive more slowly and turn on your:

A. Flashers for emergencies.
B. Parking lamps.
C. Headlights.

The right answer is C. Anytime the weather makes it difficult to see other cars, you must switch on your headlights. You may not be visible to other drivers either.

66. While driving, you should look 10 to 15 seconds ahead of you:

A. And pay attention to the center of the path.
B. Because it is required by law.
C. For early detection of possible risks

The right answer is C. Scan the highway 10 to 15 seconds before your car to see risks and prevent last-minute maneuvers. Keeping your eyes fixed on the road directly next to your car is risky.

67. To see vehicles in your blind spots, you should check:

A. The internal rearview mirror.
B. A rearview mirror on the exterior.
C. Beyond your shoulders.

The right answer is C. Blind spots are, by definition, places you cannot see in your mirrors. You should peek over your shoulder to evaluate your blind spots.

68. Which of the following statements is true?

A. It's not dangerous to drive too slowly.
B. On certain roadways, moving too slowly might be deadly.
C. Driving a car at a certain pace has no bearing on safety.

The right answer is B. When you go too slowly, other drivers may grow irritated and attempt to pass you in a hazardous manner. Driving at a legal speed while moving with the traffic is the safest option.

69. In inclement weather, you should:

A. Go off the beaten path.
B. Go through a low gear.
C. Smoothly turn and brake.

The right answer is C. When driving in bad weather, steer clear of slamming on the brakes and making sudden, fast bends. These actions will make it considerably harder to operate your car in bad weather.

70. When a school bus is stopped ahead on your side of the road with its red lights flashing, you must:

A. Drive no faster than 10 mph; slow down.
B. Halt as soon as the lights start to flash.
C. Alternate lanes while passing gently.

The right answer is B. The stop arm and flashing overhead lights are triggered when a school bus stops to load or unload kids. You are not allowed to go forward while approaching an AA bus that uses these signals till its red lights have ceased flashing, and the halt arm has indeed been retracted. Avoid driving by the way to a school that is picking up or dropping off students.

71. If bad weather makes it difficult for you to see clearly, you should:

A. Accelerate to swiftly exit the road.
B. Follow the lane that is closest to the oncoming lane.
C. Lengthen the distance you follow.

The right answer is C. Improve your following distance when visibility is compromised by darkness or bad weather. You will have more time to respond to dangers you would not otherwise perceive.

72. If a tire blows out, you should:

A. Put the brake on and keep it on.
B. Lightly use the brakes while maintaining a strong grip on the wheel.
C. Quickly make a U-turn.

The right answer is B. Hold the wheel firmly and maintain a straight course if a tire blows out unexpectedly while traveling. Put your foot off the throttle and gently use the brakes as you gradually slow down. If at all possible, avoid stopping on the road. In a secure area, pull off the road.

73. Which statement is true?

A. Turn on your cruise control to keep a consistent speed close to a railroad crossing.
B. You must halt at a railroad crossing when instructed to do so by a traffic officer or stop sign.
C. At a railroad crossing, you have the correct and are not required to stop.

The right answer is B. When a flagger, stop sign, or danger signal instructs you to halt at a railroad crossing, you must obey their instructions. When driving close to train lines, use care.

74. Which of the following statements about driving speed is true?

A. The likelihood of a fatality rises with speed.
B. Your following distance should grow as your pace increases.
C. The above two things.

The right answer is C. The likelihood of death in an accident rises as driving speeds rise. You have little chance of surviving an accident if you are traveling more quickly than 80 mph. Because driving speed increases stopping distance, you should widen your following space as you accelerate.

75. When driving in fog, it is best to drive with:

A. Headlights with high beams.
B. Headlights with low beams.
C. 4-way flashers.

The right answer is B. Use your low beam headlights when driving in snow, rain, or fog. High brightness lights may reflect off of the weather, further reducing visibility.

76. Which of these statements is true about driving and taking medications?

    A. Most cold medicines may make you sleepy, but if you take them as directed, over-the-counter medicines won't render you unable to drive.
    B. If a doctor recommends, medicines are fine to consume at any time.

The right answer is A. Always remember that taking any medication—prescription or OTC—could be harmful and affect your driving ability. Cold and allergy over-the-counter medications might make you sleepy and impair your driving ability. Knowing how your medicine affects your ability to drive is your duty.

77. You may pass a vehicle when:

    A. You are on a slope or bend.
    B. A solid line borders your lane on the road.
    C. A broken line borders your lane on the road.

The right answer is C. Drivers could cross from every lane to turn right if there is just one broken line. Passing is allowed from the lane adjacent to the broken line and not from the lane next to the solid line where there are dashed yellow lines next to solid yellow lines.

78. When using a roundabout, drivers should:

    A. Stop in the center of the roundabout.
    B. Give way to oncoming cars in the roundabout.
    C. Give way to approaching vehicles.

The right answer is B. A circle is a round crossroads with traffic moving counterclockwise around the main island and often without a traffic light. Drivers must approach the roundabout from the left, yielding to oncoming traffic, and proceed around the circle to the correct until they reach the target highway.

79. If your vehicle starts to lose traction because of water on the road, you should:

    A. Maintain a consistent pace when driving to improve traction.
    B. Use the brakes firmly to stop your car from skidding.
    C. Avoid slamming on the brakes as you gently slow down.

The right answer is C. Your tires may break all contact with the ground when traveling at speeds as high as 30 mph in severe rain and may trip up on a pool of water above the road's surface. "Hydroplaning" is the term for this. Avoid using the brakes and gradually reduce speed if your car begins to hydroplane.

80. You want to park uphill on a two-way road, and there is no curb. Which direction do you turn your front wheels?

A. Ahead of you.
B. Right, go toward the roadside.
C. Turn left and go toward the road's center.

The right answer is B. You should spin your wheels while parking, whether uphill or down on the road, without a curb, so the car will roll away from the center of the road if the brakes fail.

81. What Is the difference between traffic lights with red arrows and those with solid red lights?

A. Red arrows are only used to stop traffic that is turning.
B. Red arrows are only used for protected turn lanes.
C. You cannot turn on a red arrow, even if you stop first.

The right answer is C. When at a solid red signal, you can occasionally turn right. You may never drive left or right at a traffic signal with a red arrow.

82. When entering the interstate, check for a gap in traffic in the nearest lane, adjust your speed to match traffic, signal, and:

A. Because you have the right-of-way, you may anticipate traffic to let you move into the lane.
B. Carefully meld into the opening.
C. Before merging, wait for a lane to clear.

The right answer is B. You should locate a gap, accelerate to the flow of traffic, and signal before entering into interstate traffic. When it becomes safe to do so, merge into the gap. Keep an eye out for other vehicles, and don't rely on them to let you into the lane.

83. Is it illegal to park your vehicle?

A. In a crosswalk that isn't designated.
B. A few steps from a private driveway.
C. Inside a bike lane.

The right answer is A. Parking on a crosswalk, whether it is marked or not, is prohibited. If there isn't a sign saying, "No parking," and your car doesn't hinder a bike, you may drive in a bike lane.

84. Extra space in front of a large truck is needed:

A. To go onto the highway with other divers.
B. To halt the car, the truck turned.
C. When other drivers want to slam on the brakes.

The right answer is B. Trucks stop slower than vehicles moving at the same speed because they are bigger. Other motorists shouldn't pull out from a truck, slam on the brakes, or halt.

85. On a multilane road, a dashed yellow line next to a solid yellow line means:

A. Passing is not permitted in either direction.
B. Both directions are open to passing.
C. Only traffic from the direction indicated by the dashed line may pass.

The right answer is C. Only the vehicle immediately next to the dashed line may cross the centerline to pass if there are both solid and dashed yellow lines separating lanes of traffic. The solid line may prevent passing for drivers nearby.

86. Tailgating (driving too close to another vehicle's back bumper):

    A. It might aggravate and annoy other motorists.
    B. It cannot lead to a traffic ticket.
    C. Prevents being "cut off," which decreases crashes.

The right answer is A. Avoiding tailgating is advised since it is a prevalent practice that might result in aggressive driving. Driving recklessly might result in legal repercussions for drivers.

87. If you are continually being passed on the right and the left while driving in the center lane of an expressway, you should:

    A. Keep to the middle lane.
    B. Make your way to the alley on your right.
    C. Change lanes to your left.

The right answer is B. Drive inside the right lane unless you are overtaking or making a left turn on the road with four or more lanes and two-way traffic. Use the right-hand lane if you are traveling at a slower pace than the traffic flow on an interstate.

88. Sudden winds gusts on highways:

A. Usually only have an impact on the movement of huge trucks.
B. Only lead to visibility issues.
C. This may lead to issues with all automobiles.

The right answer is C. Strong winds may be problematic for all drivers. However, they can be particularly problematic for big trucks. Wind may reduce vision by sprinkling debris and particles onto the road, but it can sometimes actually move a car.

89. When passing another vehicle, you should return to your original lane when:

A. You can make out both headlamps of the passing car in your rearview mirror.
B. The passing car's front bumper has been cleared by your vehicle.
C. The passing car is 30 inches in front of you.

The right answer is A. Only swerve back into the original lane after passing a car when you can see its headlights in your rear view. By doing this, you can be confident that there will be space for you to safely pull back in front of another car.

90. What should you do at an intersection with a flashing yellow signal light?

A. Maintain your pace while keeping an eye out for nearby cars.
B. Cross the junction only after stopping.
C. Cross the crossing slowly and with caution.

The right answer is C. Before approaching the crossing, go slowly and pay attention. If any automobiles, bicycles, or pedestrians are at the junction, yield to them. A flashing yellow signal timing light does not require you to stop.

91. When parking your vehicle on any hill:

A. You should have one of your back wheels contact the curb.
B. Put the car in "park" and apply the parking brake.
C. If there is no curb, your front wheels should parallel the road.

The right answer is B. Always leave your car in the drive or the "park" position while parking on a slope. If there isn't a curb, you should spin your rear wheels so that if the brakes fail, the car will move out of the way from the middle of the road. If there is a curb, the front wheels must be rotated either away from and lightly touching it (if going downhill) or toward it (if headed uphill).

92. It is more dangerous to drive at night than during the day because:

A. In the darkness, your field of vision is limited.
B. The road is always more slippery at night.
C. At night, you have reduced reaction times.

The right answer is A. You cannot see as far forward at night as you do during the day due to diminished visibility and the glare of approaching headlights. When driving after dark, always use your headlights and drive carefully.

93. At dawn or dusk and in rain or snow, it can be hard to see and be seen. A good way to let other drivers know you are there is to turn on:

A. The instrument panel lights.
B. The lights in your parking lot.
C. The headlights.

The right answer is C. When visibility is compromised, and it could be challenging for other drivers to see you, you must always use your headlights. Always utilize your low beam headlights if driving conditions necessitate using your windshield wipers.

94. Large trucks turning onto a street with two lanes in each direction:

> A. Either of the traffic tracks may be used to complete the turn.
> B. Frequently need to make the turn using the left lane.
> C. Must always remain in the correct lane while turning.

The right answer is B. To make a right turn, large vehicles often need to swing wide. Due to the requirement to swing wide, a vehicle executing a right turn may initially seem to be making a left turn. When following a turning truck, pay close attention to the turn signal to determine the real direction the driver is turning.

95. You should not start across an intersection if you know you will block the intersection when the lights turn red:

A. Regardless of the situation.
B. Unless you approached the junction when the signal was yellow.
C. Unless you approached the junction when the signal was green.

The right answer is A. You shouldn't approach an intersection even if the signaling is green unless you can cross entirely well before the light turns red. You may get a citation if you obstruct the junction.

96. When turning left at an intersection:

A. Always give way to pedestrians and oncoming traffic.
B. You should give way to oncoming cars and pedestrians.
C. Never fail to give way to pedestrians and oncoming cars.

The right answer is A. Give way to pedestrians and oncoming cars while turning left at a junction. You may make the turn once the crossing is clear and the relevant lights permit.

97. If you are being followed too closely on a two-lane road:

A. To get the tailgater to pass around you, gradually reduce your speed.
B. Increase your speed to put more space between yourself and the opposing vehicle.
C. Use your brake to slow down and pick up the pace.

The right answer is A. Merge into a new lane if a motorist follows you too closely. If there isn't a lane available for entering, wait till the road in front of you is free, then gradually slow down. The tailgater will be more inclined to avoid you if you do this.

98. What does a flashing yellow traffic signal at an intersection mean?

A. The signal should be regarded as a stop sign.
B. Stop. Before crossing the crossroads, give way to all cross traffic.
C. At the approaching crossroads, slow down and pay attention.

The right answer is C. "Proceed with care" is indicated by a flashing yellow warning. Before approaching the crossroads, you should take extra caution and slow down. You should also give way to any oncoming cars, cyclists, or pedestrians, but you will not have to stop.

99. Stopping distances and the severity of collisions:

    A. Decrease when the speed of the vehicle rises.
    B. Are not impacted by how fast a car is going.
    C. Grow as the speed of the vehicle does.

The right answer is C. The repercussions of excessive vehicle speed may be catastrophic. The likelihood of significant injury and death rises as a vehicle's speed rises due to the possible impact of a collision. As your speed rises, adjust your following distance to make sure you can stop safely if necessary.

100. Blocking an intersection during "rush hour" traffic is not permitted?

    A. Unless you approached the junction when the signal was green.
    B. Regardless of the situation, even if your road is clear.
    C. Unless you have a green light or the right-of-way.

The right answer is B. If you can't cross the intersection entirely before the light turns red, you shouldn't go even if the light is green. If you obstruct the junction, you risk getting a ticket.

101. At an uncontrolled intersection where you cannot see cross-traffic until you're just about to enter the intersection, the speed limit is?

A. 15 mph.
B. 25 mph.
C. 20 mph.

The correct answer is A. A blind intersection has a 15 mph speed restriction. If there are no stop signs on any corner, and you'll see for 100 feet in each direction during the last 100 feet before crossing, a junction is deemed "blind."

102. If you come to an intersection controlled by a flashing yellow light, you must:

A. Observe the green light before moving forward.
B. Cross the crossing slowly and with caution.
C. Cross the junction only after stopping.

The right answer is B. Drivers must reduce their speed, increase their awareness, and use care when there is a flashing yellow stop sign. Watch out for pedestrians and crosswalk traffic.

103. You are on the freeway, and traffic is merging into your lane. You ought to:

A. Make space for the traffic that is merging if you can.
B. Drive more quickly to assert your right-of-way.
C. Keep your stance constant.

The right answer is A. When traffic flow allows, you should make a place for cars to enter your lane.

104. The speed limit in an alley is:

A. 20 mph.
B. 15 mph.
C. 25 mph.

The right answer is B. Any alley has a 15-mph speed restriction. Whether or whether not posted, that's always the maximum speed.

105. Which of the following statements is correct?

A. Brake using your left foot.
B. Both braking and driving your car should be done with your right foot.
C. To guarantee to stop, you should always use the brakes suddenly.

The right answer is B. Both braking and acceleration should be done with your right foot. To stop your car gradually and smoothly, you should softly press the brake pedal harder and harder.

106. Roads with double solid yellow line markings down the center indicate that passing is:

A. Permitted in both directions.
B. Permitted solely from the direction you are moving.
C. Forbidden in both directions.

The right answer is C. A double solid yellow line along the middle of the road signifies that passing is prohibited from either direction because traffic is traveling in opposing directions.

107. What is the only medically proven method of removing alcohol or other drug combinations from your system?

A. Inhale some clean air.
B. Allow your body to rest.
C. Savor a coffee.

The right answer is B. Alcohol has a rapid onset of action and a gradual elimination. Exercise, black coffee, and cold showers do not affect a person's blood-alcohol level (BAC). Your BAC can only be reduced by waiting.

108. Having a driver's license is a:

A. Right, not a luxury.
B. Not a right but a privilege.
C. Requirement.

The right answer is B. A driver's license is not a right to possess. It's a privilege that has to be kept and earned.

109. Excessive speed:

　　A. Does not raise the likelihood of a collision.
　　B. Enhances your capacity to respond to a threat.
　　C. Often leads to risky choices.

The right answer is C. One of the most frequent causes of car accidents is excessive speed. Speeding too much would not save gas and often results in risky choices.

110. Is alcohol?

　　A. A catalyst.
　　B. An antihistamine.
　　C. An antidepressant.

The right answer is C. Alcohol is a depressant that impairs your reflexes and dulls your judgment.

111. You can drive off the road to pass another vehicle:

A. If the car in front is making a left turn.
B. If traffic in your direction is divided into two or more lanes.
C. Under no circumstances and never.

The right answer is C. Never use the side to pass another vehicle on a paved or heavily trafficked section of the road.

112. Using a cell phone while operating a motor vehicle is considered a distraction because:

A. The driver starts to worry about how much the call will cost.
B. The driver's hands, eyes, and thoughts are all focused on the phone.
C. Other drivers are drawn to it as a source of attention.

The right answer is B. Because it occupies the user's eyes, hands, and thoughts, using a mobile phone and driving is risky. By using a mobile phone while driving, even the most experienced drivers increase their chance of being involved in an accident.

113. Before you change lanes, you should check your mirrors and:

A. Never take a right-shoulder glance.
B. Always slow down in your lane of traffic.
C. Take a look behind you.

The right answer is C. It is crucial to look behind you before changing lanes. To ensure you are not obstructing any cars in the sector you wish to enter, you should glance behind you. Make sure no other vehicles are trying to enter the same space before changing lanes.

114. Dim your headlights for oncoming vehicles or when you are within 300 feet of a vehicle:

A. You are coming up behind.
B. Approaching you from behind.
C. That you already succeeded.

The right answer is A. Within 500 feet of a vehicle coming toward you and 300 feet of the vehicle you are following, you must reduce your headlights to low beams.

115. You are driving on the freeway behind a large truck. You ought to:

A. Drive more closely than you would if you were following a passenger car.
B. Drive farther behind the truck rather than following a passenger car.
C. Wait to pass on the truck's right side.

The right answer is B. Because trucks have greater blind zones, you must follow a huge truck farther behind than you would if you were following a passenger car.

116. Increase your following distance when driving behind a large vehicle:

A. To more clearly view around the car's sides.
B. Because other motorists often wait to pass huge cars before pulling up beside them.
C. Because if you follow too closely, you'll be sucked into the car's slipstream.

The right answer is A. If you follow closely behind a truck, bus, van, or any other vehicle towing a camper or trailer, the driver may not be able to see you. When driving around one of these cars, widen your following distance. When driving behind one of these cars, widen your following distance. Increase your distance so you can see around the sides of the vehicle and see the road ahead since huge vehicles may also obscure your vision of the road.

117. Smoking inside a vehicle with a person younger than 18 is:

    A. It's legal if it's your kid.
    B. Always against the law.
    C. Not prohibited by the law.

The right answer is B. When a child is present, smoking in a car is always prohibited in California.

118. A distraction when driving is:

    A. Anything that makes a driver evade traffic.
    B. Anything that diverts your focus from driving.
    C. Anything that makes you concentrate more
    on driving.

The right answer is B. Anything that diverts your focus from driving while you're driving is a distraction. Distractions while driving may happen anywhere, at any time. Collisions brought on by distracted driving may result in loss of life, injury, and property damage.

119. You must notify the DMV within five days if:

A. You get a ticket for a driving infraction.
B. You sell or trade in your car.
C. Your car should be painted a unique color.

The correct answer is B. After selling or transferring the title of a car to a new owner, you are obligated by law to notify the DMV within five calendar days. Every time a title is transferred, they must be informed.

120. Adjust your rearview and side mirrors:

A. Just before you take the wheel.
B. Anytime you need them.
C. Before boarding the vehicle.

The right answer is A. What you are doing before you drive has a significant impact on your safety and the safety of many other pedestrians and drivers. You should buckle your seatbelt, adjust your mirrors, and secure anything inside or on top of your car before moving it. Never reposition your mirrors while your car is in motion.

121. Night driving presents unique problems because:

A. At night, the speed restriction is raised.
B. At night, fewer vehicles are on the roadways.
C. In the dark, it is difficult to determine
distance and vehicle speed.

The right answer is C. Driving at night has a special set of challenges for drivers. When driving at night, it may be difficult to determine the distance and the speeds of other cars due to the decreased visibility. Drivers can see only as far as the headlights allow them to.

122. If you miss your exit on the freeway, you should not:

A. Find a different path to your goal while
staying on the motorway.
B. Leave the motorway at the next exit and
return to the correct exit.
C. Turn around on the shoulder or the road.

The right answer is C. Never back up in the driving lane or on the side if you miss your exit. To the next exit or junction, keep driving. Drivers do not anticipate a car backing up in front of them on the road, which will probably result in a collision.

123. What is an important step in turning?

A. Verify all directions of traffic.
B. Accelerate more quickly.
C. Stay in the left lane at all times.

The correct answer is A. Before making a turn, you should check behind your car and both edges to ensure it is safe to go forward. To make the turn safely, reduce your speed.

124. When changing lanes on a freeway, you should:

A. Signal for at least 5 seconds.
B. Slow down before beginning to change lanes.
C. Assume your car will fit in the next lane if you signal before moving.

The right answer is A. Before lane changes on a motorway, signal at least 5 minutes in advance. Always use your turn signal to let other drivers, motorcycles, bicyclists, and pedestrians know when you are about to make a left or right turn, change lanes, slow, or stop.

125. Always carefully look for motorcycles before you change lanes because:

A. They may be difficult to notice due to their tiny size.
B. At junctions, they often have the right-of-way.
C. Motorcycles cannot share lanes with other vehicles.

The correct answer is A. When crossing roads, stay vigilant for motorbikes since their tiny size makes it easy for them to vanish into your blind zones.

126. You are approaching an intersection where a traffic signal displays a steady yellow light. If you have not already entered the intersection, you should:

A. Speed up to beat the red light.
B. Reduce your speed and proceed carefully through the intersection.
C. Come to a safe stop.

The right answer is C. You should safely stop your car at any junction with a constant yellow light. When the light turns from green to yellow while you are already at the junction, proceed through the intersection at a safe pace.

127. If oncoming headlights are blinding you while you are driving at night you should:

   A. Take a look at the road's right side.
   B. Put the high beams on your lights.
   C. Switch on and off your lights.

The right answer is A. Look to the right side of the track rather than straight ahead if the lights of an approaching car are blinding. This should keep your car on the road till you pass the approaching car safely.

128. A broken yellow line between two lanes of traffic means:

   A. The direction of travel is the same for both lanes of traffic.
   B. Passing is allowed when it is safe.
   C. Passing is prohibited.

The answer is B because single traffic lanes traveling in opposing directions are divided by dashed yellow lines. Passing is permitted when there is no approaching traffic in the fast lane.

129. You are driving on the freeway. The vehicle in front of you is a large truck. You should drive:

A. Closely behind the truck in bad weather because the driver can see farther ahead than you can.
B. Farther behind the truck than you would when following a passenger vehicle.
C. No more than one car length behind the truck so the driver can see you.

The right answer is B. When you follow a truck so closely that you can't see the driver's side-view windows, the trucker won't be able to see you and won't know you're there. Any vehicle, even trucks, should never be tailgated since doing so eliminates your margin of safety if the car next to you suddenly stops.

130. When Parking next to a curb, you should use your turn signals:

A. Just after stepping off the curb.
B. While approaching the curb but keeping a safe distance from it.
C. While approaching or backing up from the curb.

The right answer is C. When moving toward or away from the curb, drivers must indicate.

131. A blood alcohol concentration of 0.02 percent:

A. Won't affect your driving.
B. Won't put other drivers at risk.
C. It will double your chances of having an accident.

The right answer is C. A driver's probability of being in a fatal collision roughly doubles for every 0.02 percent rise in blood alcohol content.

132. When you want to change lanes, you should never:

A. Switch to a different lane while at an intersection.
B. By glancing behind you, check your blind area.
C. Verify that no other vehicles are entering the same lane.

The right answer is A. Within an intersection, you must never change lanes. Always check your blind area by looking over your shoulder before changing lanes. Pay attention to other vehicles entering the same lane.

133. It is very foggy. You should slow down and:

    A. Turn on your emergency flashers.
    B. Turn your lights to their high beam setting.
    C. Turn your lights to their low beam setting.

The right answer is C. When driving during fog, sleet, rain, or mist, use your low lights. Precipitation will reflect the intense beams of light, creating a haze and making seeing even more challenging. In addition to the low beam headlights, certain cars have fog lights that should be employed.

134. You have stopped for a train at a railroad crossing. After the train passes, you should:

    A. Wait for signal lights to stop flashing.
    B. Look for a second train.
    C. Both of the above.

The right answer is C. Be on the lookout for a second bus arriving on any track even after one has passed. Wait until all barriers have been opened and warning lights have ceased blinking before moving forward.

135. It is illegal to leave a child aged (fill in the blank) or younger alone in a vehicle:

A. Eight.
B. Seven.
C. Six.

The right answer is C. A youngster should never be left alone in a moving vehicle. A youngster under six cannot be left alone in a car unsupervised. If a person twelve years old or older is watching after the youngster, leaving them in a vehicle is acceptable.

136. If you want to pass bicyclists riding on the right edge of your lane:

A. You must blast your horn before passing the bike.
B. You cannot squeeze past the biker on a bicycle.
C. There is no excuse for passing the biker.

The right answer is B. You must, wherever feasible, leave at least 3 feet between your car and the bicycle while passing a biker. The cyclist cannot be forced off the road.

137. If you are getting tired while driving, you should:

    A. Stop, take a break, or switch drivers.
    B. Ingest a caffeinated beverage.
    C. Open a window.

The right answer is A. Take breaks every hour or so when driving a long distance to prevent the risks of driving while tired. If you can, split the driving duties with someone else so both drivers can rest while the other drives.

138. If you are being followed too closely on a two-lane road:

    A. To get the motorist to drive past you, gradually reduce your speed.
    B. Increase your speed to put more space between yourself and the other vehicle.
    C. Use your breaks to slow down, then pick up the pace.

The right answer is A. Merge into a new lane if a motorist follows you too closely. If there isn't a lane accessible for merging, wait till the road in front of you is free, then gradually slow down. The tailgater will be more inclined to avoid you if you do this.

139. Stopping distance and severity of crashes:

A. Decrease when the speed of the vehicle rises.
B. Are not impacted by the speed of the vehicle.
C. Increase with the speed of the moving object.

The right answer is C. When traffic moves at greater speeds, braking distances are greater, and collisions are more severe.

140. Which of the following factors affect an individual's absorption of alcohol?

A. Weight.
B. Height.
C. Intelligence.

The correct answer is A. A person's weight, biological sex, the volume of food in their stomach, and how many alcoholic drinks they've had all impact how much alcohol they absorb. The only way to get alcohol out of someone's blood is to wait.

141. When driving on gravel or dirt roads:

A. Compared to driving on pavement, your tires have higher traction on the ground.

B. You need to slow down since your tires don't have as much grip as they have on the pavement.

C. Compared to the pavement, visibility is improved.

The right answer is B. On loose rock and dirt roads, your tires don't have as much grip as they have on asphaltic concrete highways. You should slow down when driving over gravel or dirt. You will need more time to stop, and turning will make you far more likely to slide.

142. It is unlawful to:

A. Pass another car in any area that has a no passing sign.

B. Cross a railroad crossing after another car.

C. The above two things.

The right answer is C. When driving on slopes, in bends, or other situations when you can't see far enough ahead to pass safely, it's against the law to cross the centerline. Street crossings, railroad crossings, areas marked as no-passing zones, and areas with a solid yellow line adjacent to your lane are prohibited from passing. While the car in front of them has halted for a passenger or when traveling through construction zones, passing is prohibited.

143. To improve visibility lowered by rain or fog, drivers should use their:

A. Headlights with low beams.
B. Headlights with high beams.
C. Parking lamps.

The right answer is A. Use low beam headlights when driving in snow, rain, or fog. High beam headlights reduce vision when driving in bad weather by reflecting off the rain and back into the driver's eyes.

144. Fatigue increases the risk of:

A. Missing a doorway.
B. Missing a scheduled appointment.
C. Collision after nodding off while driving.

The right answer is C. Fatigue impairs judgment, increases the chance of a mishap, and leads to mistakes in judgments relating to speed and distance. If you are worn out, you risk falling asleep at the wheel, crashing, and hurting or killing other people.

145. The amount of alcohol in the blood is referred to as:

A. Implied approval (IC).
B. The level of alcohol in the blood (BAC).
C. Alcohol consumption frequency (RAC).

The right answer is B. The proportion of alcohol in the blood is determined by the blood alcohol concentration (BAC). The more impaired a person is, the higher the BAC number.

146. With a Class C driver's license, a person may drive:

A. A three-axle vehicle if the maximum gross mass is less than 6,000 pounds.
B. Every three-axle vehicle, regardless of weight.
C. A car towing two trailers.

The right answer is A. A three-axle vehicle must weigh no more than 6,000 pounds for someone having a Class C license to operate it.

147. Safely backing your vehicle requires all of the following:

A. As you step back, look over your right shoulder.
B. Examine the area around your car.
C. Before you turn around, sound your horn.

The right answer is C. Being unable to even see your car makes backing up unsafe. Check your surroundings for any possible dangers before getting into your car. To be alert to your surroundings when pulling out of a parking space, glance over your shoulder.

148. For which of the following traffic lights must you always stop your vehicle?

A. All traffic signals are red lights that are solid, flashing, and blacked out.
B. Flashing yellow lights and red arrows with solid red lights.
C. Flashing red lights, yellow lights, and solid red lights.

The right answer is A. A solid or flashing red light or a signal light that's also blacked out requires you to halt (not working). If the light is solid yellow, the signal will become red; if you can stop safely, do so; if not, continue with caution. Although you shouldn't stop when there is a flashing yellow light, you should continue with care.

149. To turn left from a multilane one-way street onto a one-way street, you should start your turn from:

A. Every alley (as long as it is safe).
B. The closest lane to the left curb.
C. The road in the middle of the street.

The right answer is B. You should start the move from the far left lane when turning left from one one-way street into another one-way street.

150. Must you yield to a pedestrian using a white cane or guide dog?

A. Only when the user is being guided across the street by the guide dog.
B. All the time.
C. Only when there is a crossing guard on duty.

The right answer is B. The right-of-way must always be provided to pedestrians using service animals or white canes (or without a red tip).

151. Roads are slippery after it first starts to rain. When the road is slippery, you should:

A. Avoid making turns and stops while driving at high speeds.
B. Test your tires' traction while going uphill.
C. Decrease the distance you look ahead of your vehicle.

The correct answer is A. Driving more slowly on a wet surface than on a dry road is important because a slippery, wet road prevents your tires from getting the grip they need. Avoid making sudden turns or stops to lessen the chance of skidding.

152. Always use your seat belt:

A. Unless the car was manufactured before 1978?
B. Except while riding in a limousine.
C. When seat belts are present in the car.

The right answer is C. All passengers, including minors at least 3 to 4 feet 9 inches tall and older than eight years old, must wear seatbelts, including the drivers. Even though the car has airbags, you must wear a seat belt and shoulder harness. You must utilize both the lap and shoulders belts if your car has them.

153. In rainy weather, you should be most careful when turning or stopping:

    A. After a day of nonstop rain.
    B. Thirty minutes after the rain ends.
    C. The first half an hour of the downpour.

The right answer is C. During the first half an hour of rain, you should use additional caution while turning and stopping. Since the automotive oil has not yet been removed from the pavement, the rain and oil from cars might be creating a slippery combination.

154. Two sets of solid double yellow lines two or more feet apart:

    A. May be crossed to access or leave a private driveway.
    B. Is forbidden to cross for any purpose.
    C. Need to be recognized as a distinct traffic lane.

The right answer is B. A barrier is two sets of continuous double yellow lines separated by two feet or more. This barrier may not be driven on or over, nor may a left turn or E r be made over it except at specifically marked openings.

155. If you come to an intersection and your view to the side is blocked, you should:

A. Slow down and do a double-take.
B. Maintain your pace and take a left and a right.
C. Stop and slowly go forward once you can see properly in both directions.

The right answer is C. When approaching a junction, drivers must slow down. A motorist should stop and slowly move ahead until they can see properly in both directions if their vision of oncoming vehicles is impeded.

156. When passing another vehicle, it is safe to return to your lane if you:

A. Cannot see the vehicle directly to your right.
B. See the vehicle's headlights in your rearview mirror.
C. Have passed the other vehicle's front bumper.

The right answer is B. You must make sure you are not dangerously near to the car you just passed before moving back into your original lane after passing. You may have enough space to rejoin the lane when you can see the car's headlights in your rearview mirror.

157. You are diving on a city street and see an emergency vehicle with flashing lights behind you. What should you do?

A. Drive to the right edge of the road and slow down.
B. Drive to the right edge of the road and stop.
C. Stay in your lane, slow down, and let it pass.

The right answer is B. Any emergency vehicle with its lights and siren on must be given the right-of-way. Until the emergency vehicle has passed, halt driving on the right side of the road. If you are close to a junction, go through it before stopping.

158. Is it legal to drive with an alcoholic beverage container that has been opened only if the container is

A. In front of the seat.
B. Inside the glove section.
C. Inside the trunk.

The right answer is C. Alcoholic beverage containers that have been opened must be stored in the trunk or another area where passengers cannot sit. It is particularly forbidden to have an open alcoholic beverage in the glove box. These limitations do not, however, apply to non-driving passengers in a bus, cab, camper, or motor home.

159. You should not use your horn:

A. If it is difficult to see what is ahead.
B. In case you run into another car.
C. Near pedestrians who are blind.

The right answer is C. Using your horn while driving close to a blind pedestrian might be risky. When it is safe to do so, move over for the pedestrian.

160. When driving in work zones, you should:

A. Drive closely behind the person in front of you.
B. Overtake the motorist in front of you as soon as you can.
C. Keep a safe following distance and avoid tailgating.

The right answer is C. When driving in a construction zone, maintain a safe distance from other cars, trucks, construction machinery, employees, and traffic barriers. Don't tailgate and increase your following distance.

161. When passing on the left of a vehicle, it is safe to move back into the right lane:

A. Roughly three seconds later.
B. When you can't see the car over your right shoulder anymore.
C. When the front of the car is visible in the rearview mirror.

The right answer is C. You may go back into the right lane when another car's headlights are visible in your rearview mirror while passing another car on the left. Before changing lanes, always signal.

162. Before switching on the ignition, you should:

A. Put your seatbelt on.
B. Ensure that everyone is wearing a safety belt.
C. The above two things.

The right answer is C. Establish a procedure for getting into and out of your automobile. Buckle your seatbelt and ensure all other passengers are doing the same before starting the engine.

163. When driving in fog or mist, never put your headlights on the high beam setting:

A. Your eyes will get a reflection of the light.
B. You may not be seen by approaching automobiles.
C. Behind you, cars can follow too closely.

The right answer is A. You shouldn't use your headlights on a high beam when it's cloudy or misty since the light will bounce back into your eyes.

164. To turn left from a one-way street onto a one-way street, start from:

A. The lane closest to the left curb.
B. The middle lane.
C. Any lane, if it seems to be safe to do so.

The right answer is A. Start the turn from the far left lane when turning left from a one-way street into a one-way street. Watch out for bicycles, motorcyclists, and pedestrians who may be turning left lawfully in the left lane between your car and the curb. Any available safe lane should be entered.

165. If you see orange construction signs and cones on a freeway, you must:

A. Slow down. The lane ends up ahead.
B. Be ready for employees and machinery up ahead.
C. Maintain your current pace when changing lanes.

The correct answer is B. Signs and message boards will alert you of employees, slow-moving equipment, and/or blocked lanes as you approach a construction zone. You should slow down and be ready to stop if necessary.

166. Which of the following roadways freeze first when wet?

A. Overpasses and bridges.
B. Intersections.
C. Tunnels.

The right answer is A. Overpasses and bridges often ice before the rest of the road.

167. You should always travel:

A. At the pace of the passing automobiles.
B. At the legal pace.
C. Moving swiftly, according to the road and weather circumstances.

The right answer is C. The speed you should drive your car will depend on the weather, the road, and the posted speed limit. Never go faster than the posted speed limit. If anything makes the circumstances less than perfect, slow down.

168. When turning left from a two-way street onto a one-way street, you should:

A. Enter any lane now.
B. Enter the first lane.
C. Enter the second lane.

The right answer is B. When making a turn, always move into the first legal lane closest to the direction you want to go. This indicates that you should enter the first lane when changing from a two-way to a one-way roadway.

169. You exit the freeway on a ramp that curves downhill. You should:

A. Slow down to a safe speed before the curve.
B. Slow down to the posted speed limit for the freeway.
C. Wait until you have entered the curve to begin braking.

The right answer is A. Before going around a curve, you should always slow down. Because you may not be able to see potential dangers up ahead, braking on a curve might cause your car to slide.

170. Which of the following is not a safe driving practice when driving on the interstate?

A. Slower moving vehicles must stay to the right.
B. Changing lanes without using a signal.
C. If you miss your exit, you must go to the next exit.

The right answer is B. You must always indicate when turning your car to the right or left. If traveling more slowly than the surrounding traffic on a highway, you should remain in the right lane. If you miss your exit, keep driving to the next exit since it is forbidden to turn around or reverse up on interstates.

171. Which of these is a safe driving technique?

A. In the fog, use your high beam lights.
B. Focusing on the road in front of your car.
C. Regularly check your rearview mirrors.

The right answer is C. You should scan the road and check your rearview mirrors every two to five seconds to keep alert to any risks. It's risky to look at the road in front of you all the time. Use your low beam headlights rather than your high beam headlights if you must travel in foggy situations.

172. If you can see that the roadway up ahead is covered by heavy smoke, you should:

A. Proceed after turning on your four-way flashers.
B. You should slow down, veer as far to the right as possible, and then stop off the road.
C. Turn on your high beam headlights as you proceed.

The right answer is B. If you see that the road ahead is heavily obscured by smoke, quickly slow down, veer as far to the right as you can, and come to a complete stop. Then and only then should you decide if it is safe to proceed. Remember that certain types of smoke might harm you fatally or only irritate your eyes and lungs.

173. Alcohol in any concentration is:

    A. A catalyst.
    B. An antidepressant
    C. None of those mentioned above.

The right answer is B. Alcohol is depressive at any concentration. It reduces inhibitions and slows all body processes and nerve impulses, making it difficult for users to focus and maintain their attention.

174. Which of the following driving skills are affected by the use of alcohol and/or drugs?

    A. Attentiveness and focus.
    B. Coordination and speed of reaction.
    C. Both mentioned above.

The right answer is C. Any quantity of alcohol has a depressive effect, reducing the nervous system's activity. It will impair one's awareness and concentration, lengthen their reaction time, and significantly impair coordination.

175. Changing from one lane to another is best done:

A. Swiftly and regularly.
B. As soon as a vehicle enters your blind area.
C. Cautiously and gradually.

The right answer is C. Always switch lanes gently and cautiously. Only swerve when required. A traffic collision is more likely to occur with each lane shift.

176. When planning to pass another vehicle, you should:

A. Not rely on other motorists to provide space for you.
B. Not assume that the car will let you pass if you utilize your turn signal.
C. Pretend the motorist won't change his or her pace.

The right answer is A. Never assume that you will have enough time to pass many cars at once or that other drivers will make space when you want to pass. You may have enough space to go back into your driving lane when you can see both headlights of the passing car in your rearview mirror.

177. You hit a parked vehicle and can't find the owner. What must you do?

    A. When you get home, call your insurance provider.
    B. Hold off till the owner comes back.
    C. On the parked car, attach a note with your name and address.

The correct answer is C. You must securely attach a notice with your name, contact information, and address to any parked vehicles or other property you hit.

178. If you are driving and you see animals standing near the roadway:

    A. Accelerate to frighten them away.
    B. Move cautiously and at a reasonable pace.
    C. Enter the next lane quickly.

The right answer is B. If you see animals standing close to the road, slow down and drive cautiously. They can abruptly flee or abruptly alter course. There could be other animals next to the road that are just out of sight since some animals roam in groups.

179. Which of the following statements about blind spots are true?

A. They are gone if the car has one outside mirror on each side.

B. Compared to most passenger cars, large trucks have larger blind areas.

C. By checking your rearview mirrors, you can check your blind areas.

The right answer is B. A driver's blind spots are places they cannot notice when they glance in their mirrors. Drivers of other vehicles should avoid the wide blind areas of huge trucks.

180. You should yield to a pedestrian:

A. In a crosswalk only, please.

B. Always, even if the pedestrian isn't abiding by the rules of the road.

C. Only if the traffic lights give the pedestrian the green light.

The right answer is B. Always keep an eye out for pedestrians while you are driving. Whatever the situation, you must take all precautions to avoid hitting someone.

181. If you plan to pass another vehicle, you should:

A. Not presume that the other vehicle will give you room to return to your lane.
B. Not assume the other car will let you pass if you use your turn signal.
C. Assume that the opposing motorist will keep his or her speed constant.

The right answer is A. You shouldn't assume that the area you wish to occupy is free or that other cars would grant you the right-of-way, even when you signal.

182. What usually causes a locked wheel skid?

A. Sluggish braking with excessive force.
B. Slowing down and barely braking.
C. Braking too firmly when moving quickly.

The right answer is C. The most frequent reason for a locked wheel skid is a motorist applying too much force when slowing down suddenly. Drivers should use the brakes gently and smoothly.

183. A broken yellow centerline indicates that:

A. Passing is prohibited.

B. When the path ahead is clear, passing on the right is allowed.

C. When the path ahead is clear, passing on the left is allowed.

The right answer is C. Traffic may cross the centerline to pass from your side if the yellow centerline adjacent to your side of the road is broken.

184. When there are people at the junction, and you are facing a green light:

A.You must cede the right-of-way for pedestrians.

B. You should give way to pedestrians.

C. To cross, pedestrians must wait.

The right answer is A. You must stop for pedestrians and other cars already at the junction when the signal turns green. When turning on a continuous green light, drivers must stop for pedestrians.

185. If you become drowsy while driving, you should:

    A. Attempt to resist it.
    B. Take a break.
    C. Take some caffeine supplements.

The right answer is B. Drive to the first rest area or service area you come across if you start to feel fatigued while driving to take a break, sleep, stretch, or switch drivers. Caffeine supplements and energy drinks shouldn't be used as a substitute for sleep since they may make driving much riskier.

186. It is a very windy day. You are driving, and a dust storm blows across the freeway, reducing your visibility. Should you decrease your speed and turn on your:

    A. Interior lights.
    B. Parking lights.
    C. Headlights.

The correct answer is C. Anytime road conditions make it difficult for drivers to see other cars, they must use their headlights. Dust, clouds, rain, snow, smoke, or fog on or near the highway are conditions that reduce visibility.

187. Which of these statements is true about large trucks?

    A. Compared to passenger cars, they take longer to complete.

    B. They can all stop swiftly because of their air brakes.

    C. Compared to passenger cars, they are more maneuverable.

The right answer is A. Compared to other vehicles moving at the same speed, large trucks need more time to stop. At 55 mph, the typical passenger car can come to a complete stop in 400 feet. On the other hand, a huge vehicle can stop at the same speed at approximately 800 feet.

188. You want to park downhill on a two-way road, and there is no curb. Which way do you turn your front wheels?

    A. Straight ahead.
    B. Right, toward the side of the road.
    C. Left, toward the center of the road.

The right answer is B. Turn your drive wheels toward the edge of the road while parking uphill or downhill on the road with or without a curb or when facing uphill on the road without a curb so your car will roll away from traffic if the brakes fail. To prevent rolling against the curb if the brakes fail, move your wheels toward the middle of the road while parking uphill on the road with a curb.

189. When driving behind another vehicle at night, you should:

A. Maintain the low beams setting on your headlights.
B. Use your high beam headlights until you are 10 feet from the car in front.
C. Use the high beams on your headlights.

The right answer is A. When traveling in rural regions or with no other vehicles, just use your high beam headlights. When closely pursuing another vehicle, switch your headlights to the low beam position.

190. Can you be given a speeding ticket if you drive 55 mph in a 55 mph zone?

A. Under no conditions, because it is always lawful.

B. If the terrain or the time of year call for a slower pace.

C. Only when the road is about to take a severe turn.

The right answer is B. According to California's "Basic Speed Law," you are not allowed to drive any faster than is currently safe. Though moving too quickly for the road conditions, you might still get a ticket even if your speed is within the stated limit. Drivers should consider various criteria when determining how fast to drive, including their speed, the speed of oncoming traffic, the state of the road, the presence of pedestrians and cyclists, and the weather.

191. You want to turn left at an upcoming corner. Yield the right-of-way to:

A. Oncoming vehicles also turning left.
B. All approaching vehicles.
C. Pedestrians on the sidewalk waiting for a "Walk" signal.

The right answer is B. If they have the green light to do so, you must give way to pedestrians, bicycles, and other vehicles making a left turn.

192. To help avoid skidding on slippery surfaces, you should:

A. Start descending a steep slope in a lower gear.
B. To enter bends, accelerate quickly; to depart them, decelerate.
C. Slow down before entering bends and junctions.

The right answer is C. You should slow down before entering a curve since you never know what could be there. You might slide if you brake suddenly when curved.

193. When you drive through a construction zone, you should:

A. Observe the employees by pausing.
B. Reduce the distance you follow.
C. Avoid "rubbernecking" and drive cautiously through the work zone.

The right answer is C. You shouldn't "rubberneck" to prevent adding to ongoing traffic congestion. You shouldn't take your time to look at unusual things.

194. Which of the following is true about vehicles displaying a diamond-shaped sign that indicates a hazardous load?

A. They cannot operate a vehicle on interstates.
B. Before crossing railroad tracks, they must halt.
C. They can't go faster than 35 mph.

The right answer is B. When approaching railroad lines, vehicles with signs indicating dangerous loads must stop.

195. Drivers turning left must yield to:

A. Advancing automobiles going straight ahead
or making a right turn.
B. Automobiles moving by.
C. No specific person.

The right answer is A. All cars traveling in the opposite direction must yield to vehicles making a left turn. Bicycles and motorcycles are included in this.

196. When parking uphill on a two-way street with no curb, your front wheels should be:

A. Making a left turn (toward the street).
B. Making a right turn (away from the street).
C. Similar to the pavement.

The right answer is B. You should spin your wheels while parking on a slope (either uphill or downhill) without a curb so the car will roll away from the middle of the road if the brakes fail.

197. You are required to stop your vehicle:

A. At any junction where you are told to stop by a police officer.
B. When the traffic signal is red.
C. The above two things.

The right answer is C. You must completely stop at a red traffic signal, whether it is constant or flashing. Regardless of any written signs or traffic signals, you must always abide by the directions issued by authorities controlling the flow of traffic.

198. When can you drive in a bike lane?

A. If no cyclists are using the bike lane during peak hour.
B. When you are 200 feet or less from the cross street where you want to make a right turn.
C. When you try to overtake a motorist driving right in front of you.

The right answer is B. If there is a bike lane, move into it 200 feet or less before a turn. Keep an eye out for bicycles or motorcycle riders who could cut you off from the curb.

199. If a traffic signal light is not working, you must:

A. Stop and only continue when it is safe.
B. Stop and allow all oncoming cars to pass before proceeding through the crossroads.
C. If necessary, just slack off or stop.

The right answer is A. When a traffic signal is malfunctioning and no lights are on, you should continue with caution as though stop signs are in all directions at the junction.

200. Which of the following is true about vehicles displaying a diamond-shaped sign that indicates a hazardous load?

A. They cannot operate a vehicle on interstates.
B. Before crossing railroad tracks, they must stop.
C. They can't go faster than 35 mph.

The right answer is B. When approaching railroad lines, vehicles with signs indicating dangerous loads must stop.

201. Drivers turning left must yield to:

A. Cars approaching from the right or the left, going straight.
B. Automobiles moving by.
C. No specific person.

The right answer is A. All cars traveling in the opposite direction must yield to drivers making a left turn. Bicycles and motorcycles are included in this.

202. When parking uphill on a two-way street with no curb, your front wheels should be?

A. Making a left turn (toward the street).
B. Turned to the right, parallel to the pavement, and moved away from the roadway.

The right answer is B. You should spin your wheels while parking on a slope (either uphill or downhill) without a curb so the car will roll away from the middle of the road if the brakes fail.

203. You are required to stop your vehicle:

A. Any junction where you are told to stop by a police officer.
B. When the traffic signal is red.
C. The above two things.

The right answer is C. You must completely stop at a red traffic signal, whether it is constant or flashing. Regardless of any written signs or traffic signals, you must always abide by the directions issued by authorities controlling the flow of traffic.

204. U-turns in business districts are:

A. Harmful and hence always prohibited.
B. Legal while approaching cars do not pose a risk.
C. Legal at junctions unless specifically forbidden by a sign.

The right answer is C. If a sign doesn't forbid it or there are designated turn slots, you may only do a U-turn at an intersection in a commercial area.

205. If your vehicle has a mechanical problem:

A. Enter the slow lane after giving a signal.
B. Put on your danger lights and pull over in your lane.
C. As you drive off the road, turn on your hazard lights.

The right answer is C. Make sure other cars can see your car if it breaks down on a highway. If at all feasible, pull your car off the road and away from traffic, and activate your emergency flasher to signal that you need help.

206. You must show proof of insurance to law enforcement:

A. Only in the event of a collision.
B. If you are in an accident or are being pulled over for a ticket.
C. Just if you are stopped and issued a ticket.

The correct answer is B. You must carry proof of your financial stability every time you drive, such as your insurance card. After a traffic stop or accident, you must always provide an officer with your license and proof of insurance upon request.

207. A Vehicle suddenly cuts in front of you, creating a hazard. What should you do first?

A. Honk and step on the brake firmly.
B. Take your foot off the gas pedal.
C. Swerve into the lane next to you.

The right answer is B. Take your foot off the accelerator if a car merges in front of you too closely. This will allow you to pull away from the car in front of you without slamming on the brakes or veering into another lane.

208. Give the right-of-way to any pedestrian who is:

A. In a designated crosswalk.
B. In any junction or crosswalk.
C. In any street crossing.

The right answer is C. When crossing the roadway at a marked or unmarked crosswalk; drivers are required to yield to pedestrians. Drivers should give way to pedestrians crossing any roadway out of consideration for their safety.

209. If you are facing uphill where there is no curb, set the parking brake and:

A. Your wheels should be pointed in that direction.
B. Your wheels should be turned away from the road's edge.
C. Keep the wheels pointed straight ahead.

The right answer is A. Your front wheels should be rotated to the right while parking uphill on the road without a curb (toward the edge of the road). If the brakes fail, this will guarantee that the car will skid off the road.

210. If you approach a traffic light with a red signal and a police officer directs you to go through the intersection without stopping, you should:

A. Stop as soon as the light turns red.
B. Pass past the junction without pausing.
C. Come to a full halt before moving forward.

The right answer is B. Police personnel directing traffic are always allowed to overrule official traffic signals and signage. Take the officer's instructions to heart.

211. Only ___ can lower blood alcohol concentration (BAC) and reduce alcohol's effects on a body:

    A. Drinking caffeine.
    B. Eating foods high in fat.
    C. Time.

The right answer is C. Allowing your body to clear the alcohol from your system is the only method to get sober after consuming alcohol. Nothing you do, not even eating or drinking, can speed up this process.

212. When approaching an intersection with a flashing red light, you must:

    A. Stop completely, give way to approaching cars and pedestrians, and then go forward.
    B. Slow down and be careful as you go forward.
    C. Stop completely and hold your position when the light is red.

The right answer is A. A stop sign and a flashing red traffic light have the same meaning. You must come to a complete stop and go forward once it is safe to do so while approaching a junction with a flashing red light.

213. Adjust your rearview and side mirror:

A. Just before you take the wheel.
B. Anytime you need them.
C. Before boarding the vehicle.

The right answer is A. What you do before you drive significantly impacts your safety and the safety of other drivers and pedestrians. You should buckle your seatbelt, adjust your mirrors, and secure anything inside or on top of your car before moving it. Never reposition your mirrors while your car is in motion.

214. Lines in a construction zone are:

A. Doubled.
B. Tripled.
C. Slices in half.

The right answer is A. When employees are present in road building or maintenance zones, fines for moving traffic offenses are quadrupled. Driving cautiously and following all signs, signals, police orders, and flagger instructions are required while in a construction zone.

215. Hydroplaning occurs when tires ride on a thin film of water instead of on the road's surface. To prevent hydroplaning in rainy weather, you should:

   A. Put on your cruise control to maintain a constant speed.
   B. Decrease your speed.
   C. Move to the shoulder of the road as soon as it starts to rain.

The right answer is B. You should slow down in wet conditions to lessen the chance of hydroplaning. It may be challenging to manage your car if you go too quickly since your tires may ride up on the water and lose contact with the road.

216. What does a flashing red traffic light at an intersection mean?

   A. Before entering, go more slowly.
   B. Before entering, pause.
   C. Wait for the green light and then stop.

The right answer is B. A red indicator that is flashing implies "stop." When it is safe to do so after stopping, you may go forward while adhering to all right-of-way regulations.

217. On a freezing, wet day, which of the following roadways is most likely to hide ice spots?

    A. Highways close to hilltops.
    B. Roads on overpasses and bridges.
    C. Asphalt used to pave roads.

The right answer is B. Overpasses and bridges often ice before the rest of the road. They may conceal ice patches.

218. In inclement weather, you should:

    A. Go off the beaten path.
    B. Go through a low gear.
    C. Smoothly turn and brake.

The right answer is C. When driving in bad weather, stay away from slamming on the brakes and making sudden, fast bends. These actions will make it considerably harder to operate your car in bad weather.

219. When taking any medicine, you should:

A. Before driving, discuss the consequences with your doctor.
B. Ask someone to accompany you home.
C. Drive more slowly and keep your window open.

The right answer is A. Pharmaceutical and over-the-counter legal drugs can potentially impair your ability to drive. If you have concerns about how a certain medicine or drug combination may impact your driving ability, you should always speak with your doctor or pharmacist. If your doctor writes you a prescription for a sedative or tranquilizer, you should especially make a point of speaking with them.

220. To improve visibility lowered by rain or fog, drivers should use their:

A. Headlights with low beams.
B. Headlights with high beams.
C. Parking lamps.

The right answer is A. Use low beam headlights when driving in snow, rain, or fog. High beam headlights reduce vision when driving in bad weather by reflecting off the rain and back into the driver's eyes.

221. When approaching a roundabout, you should always:

A. Accelerate more quickly.
B. Cut down on your speed.
C. Keep all the same pace.

The right answer is B. Slow down as you get closer. A roundabout is designed to be navigated slowly.

222. A broken yellow line next to a solid yellow line indicates that passing is:

A. Permitted from the side close to the solid yellow line.
B. Forbidden in both directions.
C. Permitted from the side nearest to the torn yellow line.

The right answer is C. When the center of the road is marked by a solid yellow line next to a broken yellow line, passing is permitted from the side next to the broken line and prohibited from the side next to the solid line.

223. You want to make a right turn at the corner. A pedestrian with a guide dog is at the corner, ready to cross the street in front of you. Before making your right turn, you should:

A. Turn off your engine until the person crosses the street.
B. Tell the pedestrian when to cross the street.
C. Wait until the person crosses the street.

The right answer is C. The right-of-way must always be provided to pedestrians using guide dogs or white canes (with or without a red tip).

224. To turn left from a one-way street with multiple lanes onto a two-way street, start the turn-in:

A. The lane to the very left.
B. Any open lane.
C. The lane that is closest to the center of the road.

The right answer is A. Start from the far left lane while making a left turn from a one-way street into a two-way street.

225. The speed limit at an uncontrolled railroad crossing is:

A. 25 mph.
B. 15 mph.
C. 20 mph.

The right answer is B. The speed restriction is 15 mph when you are less than 100 feet from an uncontrolled railroad crossing and cannot see the rails for 400 feet in either direction.

226. You are driving behind a motorcycle and want to pass:

A. You have to stay in the right lane as much as possible because the motorcycle is small and doesn't use all lanes.
B. Blow your horn to make the motorcycle move onto the shoulder so you can pass.
C. Have your vehicle entirely in the left lane before and during the pass.

The right answer is C. A motorbike should have a complete lane to itself while being passed. Never block the motorcycle's lane with other traffic. Too quickly entering the original lane might cause a cyclist to veer to the right, into oncoming traffic, or off the road.

227. You want to pass a bicyclist in a narrow traffic lane when an oncoming vehicle is approaching. Should you:

A. Pass the bicycle after honking your horn.
B. Slow down and let the vehicle pass you before you pass the bicyclist.
C. Wait until the bicyclist rides off the roadway.

The right answer is B. Take on one threat at a time in this circumstance. You should slow down to allow the other vehicle to pass before passing the bike when it is safe to do so, instead of attempting to squeeze between the bicyclist and the other car.

228. California's "Basic Speed Law" says:

A. Never exceed the stated speed limit when driving.
B. Never go faster than what is safe for the road conditions.
C. On several highways in California, the maximum speed restriction is 70 mph.

The right answer is B. According to the "Basic Speed Law," you should never drive faster than is currently safe. You could get a ticket for driving too fast for the circumstances if, for instance, you are driving 45 mph in a 55 mph zone during a thick fog.

229. If you pass a school bus that is stopped with its red lights flashing, you will:

A. Get a $1,000 fine.
B. Get a $100 fine.
C. Avoid any legal repercussions.

The right answer is A. When approaching a stopped school bus with its red lights flashing, vehicles must come to a full stop. If you don't stop until the red lights stop flashing, your license may be suspended, and you might be fined up to $1,000.

230. If you are getting tired while driving, you should:

A. Stop and take a break or switch drivers.
B. Ingest a caffeinated beverage.
C. Open a window.

The right answer is A. Take breaks every hour or so when driving a long distance to prevent the risks of driving while tired. If you can, split the driving duties with someone else so that you can both rest while the other drives.

231. It is legal to make a left turn at a red traffic light after stopping only if:

A. You are turning into a two-way street when you are moving into one.
B. You are turning into another one-way street as you are moving down a one-way street.
C. At the junction, you must surrender to all other vehicles.

The right answer is B. You can only turn left at a red light after coming to a full stop if you're on a one-way street and entering another one. If there are two posted signs preventing the turn, only make it.

232. You have allowed the wheels of your vehicle to run off the edge of the pavement. What should you do first?

A. To reposition the vehicle on the pavement, turn the front wheels slightly to the left.
B. Firmly grip the wheel, let off the throttle, and gradually depress the brakes.
C. Put your brakes on and quickly move your front wheels to the left.

The right answer is B. Hold the steering wheel firmly, let off the gas pedal, and gently use the brakes if your car starts to veer off the road. Wait until you move more slowly, scan the traffic, and search for a spot where you can merge safely to get back onto the road. You risk losing control of your automobile or having it enter other lanes of traffic if you overcompensate by yanking the wheel to return to the road.

233. Which of the following increases your chances of being in a collision?

A. When making a lane change, look behind you.
B. Shifting lanes to pass other cars continuously.
C. Before you begin driving, make sure your rearview mirror is adjusted.

The right answer is B. Your odds of getting into an accident increase every time you pass another car.

234. Which of the following increases your chances of being in a collision?

A. While changing lanes, keep an eye on your back.
B. Shifting lanes to pass other cars continuously.
C. Before you begin driving, make sure your rearview mirror is adjusted.

The right answer is B. You increase your risk of getting in a crash every time you pass another car.

235. To avoid hydroplaning while driving in rainy conditions, you should:

A. Drive at a speed that is suitable for the circumstances.
B. Use the brakes as soon as the automobile begins to slide.
C. Remain calm.

The right answer is C. Your tires might lose touch with the road surface if you drive too fast in a slippery environment. "Hydroplaning" is when a vehicle loses traction and rides on top of the water. Driving more slowly than you would in perfect weather circumstances while it's raining or foggy is the greatest method to avoid this.

236. If you come across livestock or other animals on the roadway, you should?

A. Be sure to move aside.
B. Stop and go slowly.
C. Neglect them.

The correct answer is B. Try to slow down and stop if it's safe to do so if you're driving and come across an animal of any sort on the road. It might be risky to make a sudden turn to avoid an animal since your car could skid and crash.

237. It is unlawful to:

A. Pass another car in any area that has a no passing sign.
B. Cross a railroad crossing after another car.
C. The above two things.

The right answer is C. When driving on slopes, in bends, or in other situations when you can see far enough ahead to pass safely, it's against the law to cross the centerline. Street crossings, railroad crossings, areas marked as no-passing zones, and areas with a solid yellow line adjacent to your lane are prohibited from passing. While the car in front of you has stopped for a pedestrian or when traveling through construction zones, passing is prohibited.

238. Which of the following are factors commonly contributing to traffic crashes?

A. Driving too quickly and going above the posted speed limit in some circumstances.
B. Getting enough sleep and being focused.
C. Observing the surroundings while maintaining attention on the job of driving.

The right answer is A. Driving too fast for the road conditions and exceeding the posted speed limit are all frequent causes of traffic accidents. Always follow the flow of traffic and obey the posted speed restrictions.

239. If there is a deep puddle on the road ahead, you should:

A. Maintain the prescribed speed to go through the water.
B. Try to stay away from the puddle.
C. Shift into neutral as you pass through the water.

The right answer is B. Avoid slippery regions, such as ice patches, wet leaves, oil, or deep puddles, to prevent skidding on slippery surfaces. A dry, firm surface is the most secure one for driving.

240. When making a right turn from a highway with two lanes traveling in your direction, you may turn from:

A. The lane that is closest to the middle of the street.
B. The lane that is closest to the road's curb.
C. Any lane depending on oncoming traffic.

The right answer is B. Start and finish the turn in the lane closest to the curb on the right. Avoid making a wide turn into a different lane of traffic.

241. At an intersection with a yield sign, you:

A. Must give way to oncoming traffic if it is near enough to be a hazard.
B. Must yield only to the cars on your right side.
C. Should reduce speed but not stop.

The right answer is A. Drivers must yield to oncoming traffic in the lanes they want to enter or cross when they see a yield sign. When approaching a yield sign, motorists should be ready to stop, but if there is no oncoming traffic, they may proceed without stopping.

242. At intersections with a "Yield" sign:

A. Crossing traffic close enough to cause a collision, you must yield the right-of-way.
B. Only cars to your right should have the right-of-way.
C. Always go more slowly and without pausing.

The right answer is A. If required, you must slow down or halt to surrender the right-of-way to vehicles merging or crossing lanes at a yield sign. Any cross traffic near enough to cause a collision must yield the right-of-way.

242. When you want to change lanes, you should never:

A. While at an intersection, switch to a different lane.
B. By glancing behind you, check your blind area.
C. Verify that no other vehicles are entering the same lane.

The right answer is A. Within an intersection, you should never change lanes. Always check your blind area by looking over your shoulder before changing lanes. Pay attention to other vehicles entering the same lane.

243. Just like alcohol and other drugs, drowsiness can:

A. Aid in making you a better driver.
B. Improve your mood.
C. Skew your judgment.

The right answer is C. Poor driving habits result from insufficient sleep. Sleepiness affects judgment, alertness, and reaction time similarly to drugs and alcohol.

244. It is dangerous to follow a motorcycle too closely because:

A. They don't adhere to the same regulations as cars.
B. A motorbike can stop significantly more quickly than an ordinary car.
C. Compared to cars, they brake more gradually.

The right answer is B. Motorcycles may stop suddenly, so following too closely puts your life and the motorcyclist's at risk. You must have adequate time and distance to prevent a collision if the motorcyclist makes a mistake.

245. Which of the following substances can affect the ability to drive?

A. Marijuana, sedatives, and tranquilizers.
B. Cold and cough medications with codeine or antihistamines.
C. The two mentioned above.

The right answer is C. Several medicines including depressants like tranquilizers and sedatives, over-the-counter cough syrups, cold remedies, and allergy treatments (which may include alcohol, codeine, or antihistamines), as well as illicit narcotics, might make it difficult for you to drive.

246. When driving at night, you should:

A. Use your high lights at all times.
B. Direct your gaze toward the approaching car with scarred headlights.
C. Lengthen the distance you follow.

The right answer is C. When it is dark and difficult to see, increase your following distance. Utilize headlights to improve visibility while adhering to the guidelines for safe usage of high and low beams. To prevent getting dazzled by the glare, avoid staring straight into an approaching vehicle's headlights.

247. Your driving lane is next to a bicycle lane. You want to make a right turn at the upcoming intersection:

A. You may not enter the bicycle lane to make your turn.
B. You should only merge into the bicycle lane if you stop before turning.
C. You must merge into the bicycle lane before making your turn.

The right answer is C. You must enter the bicycle lane while making a right turn no more than 200 feet before the corner or driveway entry. You must not operate a motor vehicle in the bicycle lane at all other times.

248. Only ___ can lower blood alcohol concentration (BAC) and reduce alcohol's effects on a body.

A. Caffeine consumption.
B. Consuming fatty meals.
C. Time.

The right answer is C. Allowing your body to clear the alcohol from your system is the only method to get sober after consuming alcohol. Nothing you do, not even eating or drinking, can speed up this process.

249. A police officer signals you to continue driving through a red light. What should you do?

A. Do as the officer tells you.
B. Wait for the green light.
C. Stop first, then do what the officer tells you.

The right answer is A. Even if it runs counter to already-existing signs, signals, or rules, you must respect any driving directions, orders, or signals provided by a traffic officer, peace officer, or fireman.

250. When driving in fog, it is best to drive with:

A. Headlights with high beams.
B. Headlights with low beams.
C. 4-way flashers.

The right answer is B. When driving in snow, rain, or fog, use your shorter wavelengths headlights. High brightness lights may reflect off of the weather, further reducing visibility.

251. Backing your vehicle is:

A. Always dangerous.
B. Dangerous if you have a helper.
C. Only dangerous in large vehicles.

The right answer is A. Being unable to see behind your car makes backing up unsafe. When backing up, use additional care.

252. You are preparing to exit the interstate. When should you start reducing your speed?

A. About halfway through the deceleration lane.
B. As you approach the deceleration lane.
C. Immediately upon entering the deceleration lane.

The right answer is C. When exiting an interstate, keep going until you reach the deceleration lane, at which time you should slow down to the stated advisory speed for the exit ramp.

253. Is it illegal to leave a child aged six or younger unattended in a vehicle on a hot day?

A. Even though kids are buckled up in a child passenger restraint device.
B. If a person twelve years of age or older is watching over them.
C. Only if the ignition is turned on.

The right answer is A. A youngster should never be left alone in a moving vehicle. A youngster under six cannot be left alone in a moving vehicle. A youngster may be left alone if someone twelve years old or older watches over them.

254. All of the following are dangerous to do while driving. Which is also illegal?

A. Wearing a headset that covers both ears.
B. Having one or more interior lights on.
C. Using cruise control on residential streets.

The right answer is A. Driving while using earplugs or a headset in either ear is prohibited.

255. At an intersection with stop signs on all corners, yield the right-of-way to any driver:

A. To the left of you.
B. Who was there ahead of you.
C. On the other side of your car.

The right answer is B. Vehicles shall go through a four-way stop after reaching a complete stop in the order they approach the junction. When more than one vehicle approaches at once, the one on the left must give way to the one on the right.

256. On a green arrow, you must:

A. Must yield to any car, bicycle, or pedestrian in the junction.
B. Yield to pedestrians only at intersections.
C. Pause for four seconds before moving on.

The right answer is A. An arrow in green denotes "go." After giving way to any cars, cyclists, or pedestrians at the junction, you must turn in the direction indicated by the arrow.

257. It is illegal for a person twenty-one years or older to drive with a blood alcohol concentration (BAC) that is ____ or higher:

A. Eight-hundredths of one percent, or 0.08 percent.
B. One-tenth of one percent, or 0.10 percent.
C. Five-hundredths of one percent, or 0.05 percent.

The right answer is A. Driving with a blood alcohol content (BAC) of 0.08 percent or more is prohibited for those twenty-one years of age or older. Alcohol use while driving is harmful and against the law.

258. When should drivers yield the right-of-way to pedestrians in a crosswalk?

A. Only if the pedestrians wave to the motorist before crossing.
B. Only if they aren't walking while texting themselves.
C. All the time.

Bring your car to a stop at a crossing to give way to any other vehicles or pedestrians already in the intersection. This is the proper answer (C). If your lane is totally clear, you may cautiously go forward.

259. You must look for bicyclists in the same lanes used by motor vehicles because they:

A. Must ride with the flow of traffic.
B. Share lanes with cars in an illegal manner.
C. Are allowed to drive alongside motor vehicles.

The right answer is C. When there is no other option and cycling is not expressly prohibited by a sign, bicyclists have the right to use the road and may legally be allowed to ride on certain motorway segments. Be on the lookout for cyclists and share the road with them when necessary.

260. Slowing down just to look at collisions or anything else out of the ordinary:

A. Congests the traffic.
B. Prevents impacts on the back.
C. Prevents collisions, hence enhancing traffic flow.

The right answer is A. Avoid "rubbernecking" or slowing down to examine crashes or other unusual events. By doing this, traffic congestion is decreased.

261. A steady green traffic light at an intersection means:

A. Increase your speed.
B. Your mirrors should be adjusted.
C. If it is safe to do so, you may go through the junction at a reasonable and safe speed.

The right answer is C. The junction may be passed through if the traffic signal is consistently green. When the junction is clear, the motorist should continue after yielding to any oncoming traffic or pedestrians.

262. How do you turn your front wheels to park downhill next to a curb?

A. Toward the curb.
B. Keep clear of the curb.
C. In line with the curb.

The right answer is A. Turn your front wheels into the curb or the side of the road while parking downward with the parking brake set.

263. As your speed increases, it is important:

    A. That your headlights should be on.
    B. To look far in front of your car.
    C. To alternate lanes often.

The right answer is B. As you go faster, it takes more time for your car to stop. When traveling fast, it's crucial to keep a good lookout for any hazards. This will give you time to safely respond.

264. A red arrow pointing to the right on a traffic light means you may:

    A. Turn in that direction after slowing down and scanning for oncoming traffic.
    B. Wait until the light turns green before turning in that direction.
    C. Turn in that direction when you come to a full halt.

The right answer is B. Stop is indicated with a red arrow. Until a green light or an arrow shows, you must remain stopped. When facing a red arrow, do not turn.

265. Before entering a curve:

   A. Set your turn signal to on.
   B. Speed up a little.
   C. Brake firmly.

The right answer is B. Depending on the state of the roads, you may travel slower than the official speed limit, but exceeding it is against the law. Driving on slippery roads, near animals and people, and approaching bends or slopes with restricted sight are a few situations that call for a slower pace for safety.

266. Having a driver's license is a:

   A. Requirement.
   B. Privilege.
   C. Right.

The right answer is B. It's important to remember that driving is a privilege and that every motorist is responsible for keeping other road users safe. The right to use that privilege could be taken away from you if you demonstrate its abuse.

267. At a railroad crossing, you must:

A. Keep an eye out for any cars that need to halt near railroad crossings (school buses, trucks carrying hazardous materials, etc.).
B. Watch out for many trains.
C. The above two things.

The right answer is C. All railroad crossings must be approached with the utmost care, and you should only go across them after being certain that no trains are headed in either direction. Keep an eye out for vehicles like school buses and trucks carrying hazardous goods that must stop at every railroad crossing.

268. What should a driver do when approaching a traffic control signal, not in operation?

A. Before approaching the junction, come to a complete stop and give the right-of-way.
B. The motorist does not need to stop if the junction is clear.
C. To avoid being hit by other cars, go through the junction fast.

The right answer is A. Unless otherwise instructed by law enforcement, a vehicle must always regard an unresponsive junction as an all-way stop and come to a full stop. The motorist must stop, look, and give way before proceeding into the junction.

269. As the percentage of alcohol (BAC) in your blood increases, you become:

A. Even drunker.
B. Extra sober.
C. More synchronized.

The right answer is A. The proportion of alcohol in a person's blood is measured by their blood alcohol concentration (BAC). The more impaired a person is, the higher their BAC.

270. Water on the road can cause a vehicle to hydroplane. Your car may hydroplane at speeds as low as:

A. 45 miles per hour.
B. 35 miles per hour.
C. 40 miles per hour.

The right answer is B. Hydroplaning occurs when standing water is on a roadway. Most tires will direct water away from the tire at speeds up to 35 mph. Beyond 35 mph, your tires won't be able to channel the water as efficiently, and you risk losing control of the vehicle and having the tires ride over the water like a pair of water skis.

271. You are approaching an intersection with a steady yellow traffic light. If you have not already entered the intersection, you should:

A. Speed up to beat the red light.
B. Reduce your speed and proceed carefully through the intersection.
C. Come to a safe stop.

The right answer is C. You should be ready to stop when a traffic signal has a constant yellow light. You should get out of the crossroads as soon as possible if you are already there.

272. You can help keep the driver behind you a safe distance away from your vehicle by:

A. Driving 10 mph quicker than the vehicle in front of you.
B. Driving 10 mph slower than the vehicle in front of you.
C. Keeping the pace constant.

The right answer is C. Keeping a safe distance behind your car might sometimes be challenging. However, by keeping a constant pace and indicating turns, lane changes, and decelerations beforehand, you may aid in keeping the motorist in front of you safe from your car.

273. When changing lanes, you should never:

A. In an intersection, cross the centerline.
B. Check your blind spots by glancing to your left or right.
C. Verify that no other vehicles are entering the same lane.

The right answer is A. Check for vehicles trying to pass you that could be attempting to join the same lane as you before changing lanes. To check your blind spot, look over your shoulder. Never try to pass or make any other lane changes at an intersection.

274. When passing another vehicle:

A. Pass the car as gradually as you can.
B. Maintain a constant speed as you pass the car.
C. Pass the car as swiftly and as safely as you can.

The right answer is C. Pass swiftly to regain vision while passing a car moving in the same direction as you. You should go back to your previous lane when you can see both of the car's headlights in your rearview mirror.

275. Which of the following statements about blind spots are true?

A. Blind spots are completely eradicated if you have a name as "mirror."
B. Compared to most passenger cars, large trucks have larger blind areas.
C. Looking in your rearview mirror can allow you to assess your blind areas.

The right answer is B. A car still contains blind spots that cannot be noticed in the outside or rearview mirrors, even if they are correctly installed. Compared to most passenger cars, big trucks have substantially greater blind areas.

276. You should drive on the shoulder to pass a car:

A. If the vehicle ahead of you is turning left.
B. Under no circumstances.
C. Suppose the shoulder is wide enough.

The right answer is B. Passing on the right is acceptable when feasible without driving off the highway. Never pass another car on the side because another motorist could pull off the road since they didn't anticipate you to be there.

277. To make a right turn at a corner, you:

A. Can't ride in the bicycle lane.
B. Alone should converge upon the bicycle.
C. You must join the bicycle lane before turning.

The correct answer is C. You must merge into the bicycle lane no later than 200 feet before the corner to perform a right turn when there is a bicycle lane. Before merging, be sure there are no bicycles in your way.

278. A solid yellow line next to a broken yellow line means that:

A. Passing is possible in both directions.
B. You may cross across the broken line.
C. You may cross the solid line nearby.

Yellow lines divide lanes of traffic traveling in opposing directions, making choice B the correct answer. You may pass if there is a broken yellow line in your driving lane.

279. When parking your vehicle parallel to the curb on a level street:

A. Turn your front wheels in the direction of traffic.
B. Eighteen inches or less must separate your wheels from the curb.
C. Your rear wheel must come into contact with the curb.

The right answer is B. Your car's front and rear wheels must be parallel to and within 25 cm of the curb while parking beside it on a level roadway.

280. When turning left at an intersection:

A. Always give way to pedestrians and oncoming traffic.
B. You should give way to oncoming cars and pedestrians.
C. Never fail to give way to pedestrians and oncoming cars.

The right answer is A. Give way to pedestrians and oncoming cars while turning left at a junction. You may make the turn once the crossing is clear and the relevant lights permit.

281. Changing from one lane to another is best done:

    A. Swiftly and regularly.
    B. As soon as a vehicle enters your blind area.
    C. Cautiously and gradually.

The right answer is C. Always switch lanes gently and cautiously. Only swerve when required. A traffic collision is more likely to occur with each lane shift.

282. To know where traffic is behind you:

    A. Keep checking your rearview mirror.
    B. Turn around and glance out the rear window.
    C. Avoid letting other cars into your blind areas.

The right answer is A. To keep track of the location of cars behind them, drivers should often check their rearview mirrors.

283. When merging onto the freeway, you should be driving:

A. At or close to the motorway traffic speed.
B. At the permitted pace.
C. Slower than the flow of traffic on the motorway.

The right answer is A. Unless the traffic moves faster than the posted speed limit, you should join a highway at or close to that speed.

284. You must yield the right-of-way to an emergency vehicle that is using its siren and flashing lights by:

A. Driving as near as possible to the right side of the road and halting.
B. Driving slowly till it passes while switching to the right lane.
C. Stop right away, even if you are at an intersection.

The right answer is A. Any emergency vehicle with its siren and flashing lights must be given the right-of-way. Take caution not to halt at an intersection when you drive to the right edge of the road and stop. Once the emergency vehicle has passed, you may move once again.

285. To prevent tailgating, drivers should follow the?

    A. Rule of one second.
    B. Rule of two seconds
    C. Rule of three seconds.

The correct answer is C. Tailgating is the main factor in most rear-end incidents. Just use the "three-second rule" to prevent tailgating. Count "one-thousand-one, one-thousand-two, one-thousand-three" when the car in front of you passes a certain location, such a sign. You are going way too fast if you cross the same location before you have finished counting.

286. You shouldn't abruptly stop in front of big trucks and buses due to the following reasons:

    A. Large trucks and buses are difficult for drivers of little cars to see in their rearview mirrors.
    B. Due to their size and weight, large trucks and buses need greater stopping distances than smaller passenger cars.
    C. Large buses and trucks move faster than tiny cars and trucks.

The correct answer is B. It takes longer distances for large cars to stop and accelerate than for small ones. It's risky to make an abrupt halt in front of a big car since the other driver may not be able to stop quickly enough to prevent a collision.

287. You have been involved in a minor traffic collision with a parked vehicle and can't find the owner. You should:

A. Leave a note on the vehicle.
B. Report the collision without delay to the city police or, in unincorporated areas, to the California Highway Patrol.
C. Both of the above.

The right answer is C. If you collide with a parked vehicle or another object, place a note with your name, contact information, and address to the object you struck. You must report the accident to the local police department or the California Highway Patrol if it occurred in an unincorporated region (CHP).

288. If weather or light conditions require you to have your lights on while driving:

A. Utilize the parking lights.
B. Activate your high beams.
C. Utilize the low beams.

The right answer is C. When driving in foggy, snowy, or wet weather, use your low beam headlights. High beam headlights will bounce back light, creating glare and making it much harder to see in front of you.

289. Which of the following is true about roadways on bridges and overpasses in cold, wet weather?

A. They often experience freezing before the rest of the road.
B. Because they are built of concrete, they do not freeze.
C. They usually begin to ice before the rest of the road.

The right answer is A. Overpasses and bridges often ice before the rest of the road. They may conceal ice patches.

290. When entering traffic after being parked at a curb, you:

A. Should move 200 feet slower than regular traffic.
B. Should pause until there is sufficient space between vehicles before accelerating.
C. Should not enter the lane until the first two cars have passed.

The right answer is B. You should always wait for a break in traffic before accelerating into city or road traffic. This will allow your car to catch up to the flow of other vehicles.

291. Use your headlights on rainy, snowy, or foggy days:

A. To keep your engine warm.
B. So others can see your vehicle.
C. To warn others of bad weather conditions.

The right answer is B. It could be hard for other drivers to see your car on wet, snowy, or foggy days. Headlights let drivers see your car more easily in these circumstances. You must also switch on your low beam lights if the weather allows you to use your windshield wipers.

292. Check your rearview mirrors:

A. Often to monitor the flow of traffic
behind you.
B. To see whether a car is in your blind area.
C. Just while you are accelerating.

The right answer is A. Avoid staring fixedly out the window while driving. Check your rearview mirrors often to track nearby cars' whereabouts.

293. If you drive faster than other vehicles on a road with one lane moving in each direction and continually passing the other cars, you will:

A. Get there considerably faster and in a safer manner.
B. Increase the likelihood of a collision.
C. Aid in avoiding traffic congestion.

The right answer is B. On two-lane roads, overtaking other cars is discouraged. Your chances of colliding with a car rise every time you leave one.

294. You should signal continuously while turning and because of it:

A. Before completing a turn, switching off your signal is against the law.
B. Inform other drivers of your intentions.
C. Switching off a sign before finishing a turn is never a good idea.

The right answer is B. To let other motorists, motorcycle riders, bicyclists, and pedestrians know your intentions, you should always signal before turning, changing lanes, slowing down, or stopping.

295. Should you turn on your headlights?

A. Thirty minutes after dusk.
B. When a train crossing is blocked.
C. While a school bus is parking.

The right answer is A. When using windshield wipers because of rain or snow or in any other circumstance when eyesight is less than 1,000 feet, headlights must be utilized from one-half hour after nightfall until one-half hour before dawn. Even in warm weather, they should be utilized whenever a vehicle is driving on a narrow rural or mountain road.

296. You are approaching an intersection with a steady yellow traffic light. If you have not already entered the intersection, you should:

A. Speed up to beat the red light.
B. Reduce your speed and proceed carefully through the intersection.
C. Come to a safe stop.

The right answer is C. You should be ready to stop when a traffic signal has a constant yellow light. You should get out of the crossroads as soon as possible when you're already there.

297. A vehicle stopped on the right shoulder of the road with its hazard lights on. Should you?

A. Change lanes to the left and speed up.
B. Slow down and pass very carefully.
C. Stop your vehicle until you can see what has happened.

The right answer is B. Slow down if you see a car's hazard lights up ahead. An accident or other kind of traffic issue might be up ahead. If someone asks for help, stop and provide it; otherwise, proceed with extreme caution.

298. You just sold your vehicle. You must notify the DMV within ____days:

A. Five.
B. Ten.
C. Fifteen.

The DMV must be notified within five days of car sales or transfers. Thus option A is the correct answer.

299. If you are driving near a large commercial vehicle, you should:

A. Closely follow the big vehicle to minimize wind resistance on your vehicle.
B. Avoid spending a lot of time driving next to it.
C. Drive on your right side when on bends and slopes.

The right answer is B. You would avoid driving next to big commercial trucks for extended periods since they have significant blind zones on either side.

300. If you are involved in a traffic collision, you are required to complete and submit a written report to the DMV:

A. Only if either you or the other driver suffers harm.
B. If there are any injuries or property damage worth more than $1,000.
C. Just in case you're to blame.

The right answer is B. Each motorist involved in an accident must submit a report to the DMV within ten days if there is a fatality, serious injuries, or property damage totaling more than $1,000. A driver's insurance agent, broker, or legal representation could submit the report on their behalf in specific circumstances.

301. Always stop before crossing railroad tracks when:

A. You can't cross the tracks entirely to the other side since there isn't enough space.
B. There is a lot of train traffic in the city or town where the railroad crossing is situated.
C. You are driving a passenger vehicle while carrying two or more small children.

The right answer is A. Trains may be expected to run on any track at any time or direction. You should wait until you can cross the tracks entirely if you need to halt after crossing them. Before you stop, be sure your car has cleared the tracks.

302. Double solid yellow lane markings mean that:

A. Both lanes are immobile.
B. Both lanes might move.
C. Right-hand lanes may pass.

The right answer is A. When two lanes of traffic are moving in different directions, they are separated by yellow lane lines. Passing is banned from both directions where double solid yellow lanes lines exist.

303. When approaching an intersection that is controlled by a flashing red traffic signal, you must:

A. Stop completely, give way to oncoming vehicles or pedestrians, and then go forward.
B. Slow down and be careful as you go forward.
C. Stop completely and hold your position when the light is red.

The right answer is A. As you would regard a stop sign, obey flashing red traffic lights. Stop completely, give way to oncoming vehicles or people, and then go forward when it is safe.

304. Alcohol is:

A. A catalyst.

B. An antihistamine.

C. An antidepressant.

The right answer is C. Alcohol is a depressant that impairs your reflexes and dulls your judgment.

305. Which of the following describes the thinking of defensive drivers?

A. They are certain that other drivers will act morally.

B. They anticipate possible actions from other motorists and are ready to respond.

C. They provide more and don't wait for breaks.

The right answer is B. Defensive driving involves foreseeing probable mistakes committed by other drivers and planning to make up for such faults.

306. Motorcycles, scooters, and mopeds are not easy to see. Therefore:

A. When driving, go slowly.
B. Keep an eye out for anything.
C. Give a motorcyclist a lane.

The right answer is B. Due to their diminutive size, motorcycles are often overlooked or readily camouflaged in a car's blind zone. Automobile drivers must always look for motorcycles, mopeds, or scooters.

307. To improve visibility lowered by rain or fog, drivers should use their:

A. Headlights with low beams.
B. Headlights with high beams.
C. Parking lamps.

The right answer is A. Low beam headlights must be utilized when driving in wet or foggy conditions. Low beams can make it simpler for other people to see you, even if they don't do much to assist you to see.

308. You should not use your horn:

    A. If it is difficult to see what is ahead.

    B. In case you run into another car.

    C. Near pedestrians who are blind.

The right answer is C. Using your horn while driving close to a blind pedestrian might be risky. When this is safe to do so, move over for the pedestrian.

309. If you are driving near a large commercial vehicle:

    A. To minimize wind resistance on your vehicle, closely follow the big vehicle.

    B. Avoid spending so much time driving next to it.

    C. When on bends and slopes, drive on your right side.

The right answer is B. You should stop driving next to big commercial trucks for extended periods since they have significant blind zones on either side.

310. Will placard abuse result in?

A. Revocation of cards alone.

B. Only a nice.

C. Revocation of the badge, a fine, and/or a prison sentence.

The right answer is C. It is a misdemeanor to misuse a placard or plate for the handicapped. Placard misuse carries a maximum $1,000 fine and a maximum six-month prison sentence in addition to the loss of all special parking privileges.

311. When driving at night, you should:

A. Use your high lights at all times.

B. Direct your gaze toward the approaching car's headlights.

C. Lengthen the distance you follow.

The right answer is C. Driving at night is riskier than driving during the day since it is more difficult to gauge speed, distances, and other possible dangers due to the reduced visibility. If the car in front of you should suddenly stop, widen your following distance to avoid a collision. When driving at night, use your headlights according to the safe high-beam and low-beam operation guidelines.

312. On rainy, snowy, or foggy days, turn on your windshield wipers and use your headlights:

    A. In the high beam position.
    B. So other drivers may see you.
    C. Just while using the highway to travel.

The right answer is B: When it's overcast, rainy, snowy, or foggy, turn on your headlights. You must activate your lower energy headlights whenever the weather calls for you to utilize your windshield wipers.

313. Flash your brake lights or turn on your emergency flashers if:

    A. There is a need to alert oncoming traffic about a collision.
    B. You are making a delivery while momentarily parked in a lane of traffic.
    C. You are leaving a parking place by backing up.

The right answer is A. If you can see an accident coming, flash your emergency lights or swiftly press the stop pedal three or four times to alert the cars behind you.

314. If you are feeling fatigued while driving:

A. To get where you're going faster, pick up the pace.
B. Your radio's volume should be raised.
C. To take a quick snooze, locate a secure parking space.

The right answer is C. Keep an eye out for tiredness warning signals while driving. If you are having trouble keeping your eyes open, swerving from your lane, or cranking up the radio and pulling down your windows to stay alert, you are too sleepy to drive safely.

315. You are driving on a one-way street. You may only turn left onto another one-way street if:

A. You increase your speed before the turn.
B. Traffic on the street moves to the right.
C. Traffic on the street moves to the left.

The right answer is C. Since there is no sign banning the turn, you may turn left into a one-way road that travels to the left. Turning left into a one-way street with right-moving traffic is not permitted.

316. When may you legally drive around or under a railroad crossing gate?

A. Never.
B. When both directions are seen clearly.
C. While none of the danger lights is blinking.

The right answer is A. Don't go around or under any lower gates at a railroad crossing. Once the gate is open, wait until you can see well in both directions and ensure no trains are approaching before crossing the tracks.

317. A U-turn is not permitted:

A. Inside a garage.
B. Everywhere there is a slope or bend.
C. Five hundred feet in each direction with unobstructed visibility on a straight stretch of road.

The right answer is B. Never turn around when on or very close to a curve or slope. You might be unable to detect approaching vehicles or people, which might result in an accident.

DRIVE WITH ME TO: CALIFORNIA DMV HANDBOOK | 201

318. At a railroad crossing, you must:

A. Keep an eye out for any cars that need to halt near grade crossings (school buses, trucks carrying hazardous materials, etc.).
B. Watch out for many trains.
C. The above two things.

The right answer is C. All railroad crossings must be approached with the utmost care, and you should only go across them after being certain that no trains are headed in either direction. Keep an eye out for vehicles like school buses and trucks carrying hazardous goods that must stop at every railroad crossing.

319. At intersections, crosswalks, and railroad crossings:

A. Always take a moment to reflect before moving slowly.
B. To notice what is approaching, look to the sides of your car.
C. Pass slowly through traffic that seems to be idly parked.

The right answer is B. You should always check the left and right sides of your car to ensure no one is approaching whenever you approach a location where people could cross or join your route or where one line of traffic meets another.

320. If your vehicle has a two-part safety belt system, you should:

A. Just wear your lap belt.
B. Utilize the shoulder and lap belts.
C. Just wear your shoulder belt.

The right answer is B. Wear both the lap and shoulder belts if your vehicle has two different seat belt systems. Your protection is significantly reduced if you wear either belt alone. Make sure to fasten your seatbelt if your shoulder belt is automated.

321. You may cross double yellow lines to pass another vehicle if the:

A. Vehicle in front of you moves to the right to let you pass.
B. Yellow line next to your side of the road is broken.
C. Yellow line next to the opposite side of the road is broken.

The right answer is B. If there is a broken yellow line inside the middle of the road, motorists may pass if it is safe to do so.

322. If pedestrians are illegally crossing in the middle of the street instead of in a crosswalk, you:

A. Should stop for them.
B. Don't need to wait for them.
C. Ought to horn-honk at them.

The right answer is A. At all times, you must stop for pedestrians. You must still stop for pedestrians even if they are jaywalking and crossing the roadway against the rules.

323. You reach an intersection with stop signs on all four corners simultaneously as the driver on your left. Who has the right-of-way?

A. The driver on your left has the right-of-way.
B. You have the right-of-way.
C. Whoever is signaling to make a turn has the right-of-way.

The right answer is B. The car to the right has the right-of-way if two vehicles approach a junction with stop signs on each corner simultaneously.

324. You must stop at the intersection ahead. Just before the intersection, you have to cross railroad tracks. You should stop before crossing the railroad tracks. When?

A. There isn't room on the other side for you to completely cross the tracks.
B. The crossing is located in a city or town with frequent train traffic.
C. You are transporting two or more children in a passenger vehicle.

The right answer is A. You should wait until you can cross the tracks entirely if you need to halt after crossing railroad tracks. Before you stop, be sure your car has cleared the tracks.

325. You drive defensively when you:

A. Distance yourself from the automobile in front by one car length.
B. While driving, focus only on the vehicle in front of you.
C. Keep moving your eyes to scan for any potential dangers.

The right answer is C. When you scan the horizon for possible dangers, you exercise defensive driving. It's risky to stare at the road immediately next to your car. Keep an eye out for nearby automobiles as you survey the horizon.

326. You must file a report of a traffic accident occurring in California. When?

A. A smog test on your car is negative.
B. An accident involves you, and someone gets hurt.
C. You switch your insurance provider.

The right answer is B. If someone was hurt (even slightly) or died in an accident, you must notify the DMV within ten days. Whether or not you caused the accident, even if it happened on private land, you or your agent must file this report.

327. When can you drive in a bike lane?

A. Thirty minutes after dusk or 30 minutes before dawn.
B. When vision is poor because of fog.
C. Two hundred feet are needed before the turn.

The right answer is C. You must approach the bicycle lane while making a right turn no more than 200 feet before the corner or driveway entry. At any other time, do not care in the bicycle lane.

328. Which of these vehicles must always stop before crossing railroad tracks?

    A. Tankers with signs warning about dangerous chemicals.
    B. A boat trailer being towed by a pickup truck or an RV.
    C. Sport utility vehicles that can accommodate four or more people.

The right answer is A. A diamond-shaped sign on a truck indicates that the cargo is possibly hazardous (containing gas, explosives, etc.) These signs mandate that cars stop before they cross railroad lines.

329. When driving on a slippery surface, such as snow or ice:

A. Before descending steep slopes, change into a low gear.

B. Follow other cars carefully to maintain traction.

C. To prevent your brakes from freezing, pump them.

The right answer is A. You should change to second gear before descending a steep slope to avoid skidding in slippery conditions. Additionally, you should follow the car in front of you more closely than usual. Avoid making abrupt stops. Push the brakes to slow down or stop if you don't have antilock brakes.

330. A large truck is ahead of you and is turning right onto a street with two lanes in each direction. The truck:

A. May complete its turn in either of the two lanes.
B. May have to swing wide to complete the right turn.
C. Must stay in the right lane at all times while turning.

The right answer is B. The rear wheels of a vehicle revolve on a shorter route than the front wheels. The separation between the front and proof tracks increases with vehicle length. As a result, making a right turn requires lengthy trucks to swing wide.

331. If a road is slippery, maintain the following distance that is:

A. Nothing out of the ordinary.
B. A little farther than usual from the automobile in front.
C. More closely than usual to the car's head.

The right answer is B. On a slippery road, you need more space to stop your car than on a dry one. When driving on slippery roads, keep a greater following distance.

332. If you argue with another person and you are angry:

A. Play the radio loudly while driving to avoid thinking about your disagreement.
B. Before you drive, let yourself cool down for a while.
C. To release tension, go to the highway.

The right answer is B. Your ability to drive safely is affected by your emotions. Give yourself some time to cool before driving if you are furious, thrilled, scared, anxious, or sad. Without thinking about the things that irritate you, you must be able to concentrate on driving.

333. You can help keep the driver behind you a safe distance away from your vehicle:

A. Driving 10 mph faster than the vehicle in front of you.
B. Driving 10 mph slower than the vehicle in front of you.
C. Keeping the pace constant.

The right answer is C. Keeping a safe distance behind your car might sometimes be challenging. However, by keeping a constant pace and indicating turns, lane changes, and decelerations beforehand, you may aid in keeping the motorist behind you as far away from your car as is safe.

334. A peace officer signals you to drive to the edge of the roadway. You decide to ignore the officer's warning and flee the scene. You are guilty of a misdemeanor and can be punished by being:

A. Fined up to $ 1,000.
B. Jailed in the county jail for not more than one year.
C. Given a warning and citation.

The right answer is B. Anyone who intentionally flees or tries to elude a peace officer from doing their responsibilities while driving a motor vehicle is guilty of a misdemeanor and punished by up to a year in county jail.

335. Animals may be transported in the back of a pickup truck only if:

A. The truck bed's sidewalls are at least 18 inches tall.
B. They are securely fastened.
C. The truck's tailgate is closed.

The right answer is B. If an animal is not adequately restrained to prevent it from falling, leaping, or being thrown from the vehicle, it may not be carried in the back of a pickup or other truck.

336. What is the benefit of a space cushion around your vehicle?

A. The traffic flow may be improved by other automobiles cutting before you.
B. You have time to respond if another motorist makes a mistake.
C. In the event of a collision, it inflates to shield you from harm.

The right answer is B. Maintaining distance around your car is crucial to giving yourself enough time to respond safely if another driver makes mistakes. For instance, having more room around your car may allow you to stop or move out of the path of a car that is about to swerve into your lane.

337. If you are driving and the rear end of your car starts skidding to the left, you should:

A. Make a right turn.
B. Make a left turn.
C. Put the car in neutral and softly tap the brakes.

The right answer is B. Take your foot off the brake if your car starts to skid, and then turn the wheel in the desired direction. For instance, you should steer left if the back of your car is swerving to the left. This will assist in aligning the front and rear of the car, straightening the vehicle's general direction.

338. If the driver of an oncoming vehicle fails to dim their headlights:

A. In front of you, scan the middle of the street.
B. Take a look at the right side of the street.
C. Look straight forward.

The right answer is B. Look to the correct side of the road if an approaching car doesn't turn off its headlights. You'll be able to see enough of the road to remain on course and avoid getting dazzled by the other car's headlights. Don't attempt to respond by keeping your lights on bright.

339. A broken yellow line next to a solid yellow line indicates that passing:

A. From the side close to the solid yellow line is permitted.
B. In both directions are forbidden.
C. From the side nearest to the broken yellow line is permitted.

The right answer is C. Passing is allowed from the side adjacent to the broken line and is banned from the side next to the solid line when the center of the road is delineated by a solid yellow line next to a broken yellow line.

340. The best thing to do if you become tired while driving is to:

A. Take a break or switch drivers.
B. Savor a coffee.
C. Open a window.

The right answer is A. Changing drivers or stopping driving is preferable if you start to feel fatigued while driving. Driving becomes dangerous when you're weary since it makes your thinking sluggish and delays your reflexes.

341. If the roadway is wet or icy, you should:

A. Speed up a little.
B. Follow the stated speed limit.
C. Hurry up.

The right answer is A. You should slow down if the street is wet or icy because your tires won't grip the pavement as well in those conditions as in dry ones.

342. At an intersection with stop signs on all corners, yield the right-of-way to any driver:

A. To the left of you.
B. Someone who was there ahead of you.
C. On the other side of your car.

The right answer is B. Cars shall go through a four-way stop after reaching a complete stop in the sequence in which they arrive at the junction. If many vehicles arrive at once, the vehicle on the left must give way to the vehicle on the right.

Made in the USA
Las Vegas, NV
05 January 2024

83757460R00118